GW01339637

PILATES
INCORPORATING 'CHI' PRINCIPLES

SANDIE KEANE

Acknowledgments:
Modelling and specialist advisor:
Sandie Keane, qualified STOTT Pilates Mat instructor
Teacher Trainer in Pilates & Mind Body Fitness.
Models: Sandie Keane, Debbie Keane, Steve Wright and Louise Bennett.
Photographs taken at 'The Waterside Lodge' Southport.

Photography:
Charles Walker Photographic p. 40

Published in 2002 by Caxton Editions
20 Bloomsbury Street
London WC1B 3JH
a member of the Caxton Publishing Group

© 2002 Caxton Publishing Group

Designed and produced for Caxton Editions
by Open Door Limited, Rutland, United Kingdom

Editing: Mary Morton
Setting: Jane Booth
Digital Imagery © copyright 2002 PhotoDisc Inc.

All rights reserved. No part of this publication may be reproduced or transmitted in any form or by any means, electronic or mechanical, including photocopying, recording or any information storage and retrieval system, without prior permission in writing from the copyright owner.

Title: Pilates, Incorporating 'Chi' Principles
ISBN: 1 84067 392 3

IMPORTANT NOTICE:
This book is not intended to be a substitute for medical advice or treatment. Any person with a condition requiring medical attention should consult a qualified medical practitioner or therapist.

PILATES

INCORPORATING 'CHI' PRINCIPLES

SANDIE KEANE

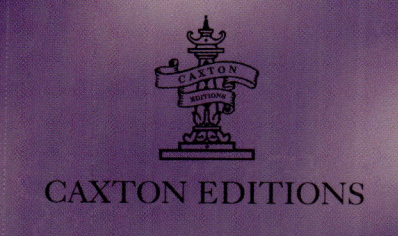

CAXTON EDITIONS

CONTENTS

CHI PILATES — 6

LOOKING AT POSTURE — 12

'LENGTHENING' AS OPPOSED TO STRETCHING — 16

POSTURAL SCENARIO — 17

SELF-POSTURAL ANALYSIS — 19

OSTEOPOROSIS AND PILATES — 21

CHI PILATES PRINCIPLES — 22
- BREATHING — 23
- PELVIC ALIGNMENT AND STABILITY — 27
- RIBCAGE PLACEMENT — 32
- SCAPULAR MOVEMENT — 32
- HEAD AND CERVICAL SPINE PLACEMENT — 34

POSTURAL POSITIONS — 36

LOOKING AT THE DEEPER PICTURE – EAST AND WEST RE-UNITED — 41

PILATES EXERCISES — 56
- EXERCISE REQUISITES — 56
- BALANCE — 58
- FORWARD ROLL — 59
- SEATED TWIST AND TILT — 60
- LYING ON YOUR BACK... — 61
- WARM-UP – ON THE FLOOR — 62
- ANKLE CIRCLES — 64
- SPINAL FLEXION — 65
- KNEE LIFTS — 66
- THE HUNDRED — 67
- SHOULDER BRIDGE — 69
- ROLL-UP — 71
- LEG CIRCLES — 73
- INNER THIGHS — 73
- LEG LIFTS (SINGLE-LEG PREPARATION EXERCISE) – — 74
- SINGLE-LEG STRETCH — 75
- OBLIQUES — 76
- DOUBLE-LEG STRETCH — 78

CONTENTS

SIDE-LYING HIP EXTENSION	79
LEG EXERCISES	80
HAMSTRING STRETCH	81
ROLL-DOWN	82
HIP ROLLS	83
LIZARD	85
STAR	86
PRESS-UPS	87
BREAST STROKE	89
SWAN DIVE	90
TABLE BALANCE	92
ARM CIRCLES	93

INDEX 94

CHI PILATES

FOREWORD

The Pilates method of exercise has been a well-kept secret until recently when those outside the dancing and acting profession, myself included, having experienced the benefits, have taken it upon themselves to share their findings with those wanting to learn. Within the fitness industry, Pilates is now one of the most sought-after fitness programmes of the 21st century.

Below: Pilates is now one of the most sought-after fitness programmes of the 21st century.

It is not a quick fix method for toning up the body, nor is it a fad. This method has impressed other fitness leaders, physiotherapists and osteopaths sufficiently for them to learn and to include the techniques in their own practice.

The discipline of this method is akin to the disciplines of T'ai Chi Chuan, Chi Qong and yoga. The focus on the breath and the centre of the body is also profoundly similar to the Eastern philosophies relating to health and well-being.

I have included the word 'chi' in the title because in China 'chi' can be translated as 'vital energy', 'life force' or 'breath'. These words are descriptive of some of the benefits you gain from following the Pilates method. General Pilates focuses on core stability. Chi Pilates includes the mind, body and spirit element, and tapping into our internal energies through exercise.

The East has been working with internal energy for thousands of years, but it is only now that we in the Western world are acknowledging its existence and its powerful properties. Chi is unseen energy. In the West we observe energy through electric, atomic or mechanical forms. In the East chi is seen in the air, in the body and in food. In Japan it is called Ji and in India Prana.

CHI PILATES

Whatever way you wish to view this energy, we are all aware of its presence. We can see and feel it in a storm in the form of lightning; we feel it in the sense of excitement or fear. Without our chi, life force, breath, we die. The quality of our breath, our food and our exercise has a direct effect on our internal and external being. By combining the knowledge of the East and the West we can nurture our entire being.

Alternative medicines, therapies and exercise disciplines are in more demand now than ever before because people are beginning to take control of their lives and turning back to nature's remedies for solutions to problems. The greatest teacher is our own body – if we only take the time to listen to it.

> *By the age of 40 man should be his own physician.*
> William Shakespeare

JOSEPH PILATES

Unlike the Eastern disciplines, Pilates is relatively new, having come to England in the 1920s via a German gymnast and athlete called Joseph Pilates. He studied and worked with Eastern and Western philosophies and formed his own technique. He came to England to train detectives at Scotland Yard, but during the war was interned. He continued to train his fellow internees and also helped those who were bedridden by making devices that would attach to their beds in order for them to train. After the war he moved back to Germany but, when asked to train the German army, he decided to leave for America. He met his wife Clara on the journey over and they opened the first Pilates studio in New York. His studio attracted top ballet dancers, actors and athletes, some of whom went on to teach others and his disciples grew. Pilates would tailor an exercise programme for the individual and, if necessary, would make specific equipment so they could achieve their greatest potential. Using his principles, Pilates teachers today are able to adapt or modify an exercise for their own clients.

The exercises in this book include modifications, benefits and watch points for your attention. However, I would like to stress that full benefits are achieved by attending a session given by a qualified teacher as they can assess your posture and your requirements. Books and videos should be used as sources of reference to practise what you have been taught under supervision.

Above: Pilates teachers today are able to adapt or modify an exercise for their own clients.

CHI PILATES

MOST COMMON QUESTIONS ASKED ABOUT CHI PILATES

Below: an abdominal curl. On the curl-up the emphasis would be on lengthening the spine, and on the way down on lengthening the abdominals.

How do you pronounce Pilates?

Pilates is pronounced 'pill-r-tees'.

How do you pronounce 'chi'

Pronounce the 'ch' as you would in the word **church**. The 'i' is pronounced 'ee' – 'chee'.

What is Pilates?

Pilates is a health and fitness programme to re-align and strengthen the body.

Why is it different to other fitness disciplines?

The focus is on re-alignment of the body and stabilising the muscles that support the spine. The emphasis is on the lengthening process rather than the shortening.

e.g. An abdominal curl – on the curl-up the emphasis would be on lengthening the spine, and on the way down lengthening the abdominal

Who is this programme designed for?

Everyone can benefit from Pilates, because the exercises are done with precision. You should not experience any discomfort or pain. You work within your own range of movement, slowly increasing that range as the fibres within the muscles start to lengthen. The changes within the body are very subtle and you do not notice them initially. However, the benefits are profound and you can start accumulating those benefits from the first session.

How many times a week should you do this?

Pilates is a lifestyle, so the principles should be worked with every day in every situation. The exercises realign, lengthen and strengthen any imbalances so how often you do them depends on what you want to achieve.

A general guideline is to do a little and often.

What benefits do you get from Pilates?

- *Pilates will improve your posture, and you can regain lost height.*

- *It will improve the strength of the muscles, which will improve their tone.*

- *Strong muscles are beneficial to supporting the skeleton more efficiently.*

- *Improved flexibility is accompanied by an increase of mobility within the joints, allowing freer movement*

- *The breathing helps the efficiency of the lungs, circulation, and blood supply to the muscles.*

- *Improved concentration and reduced stress levels.*

- *From a Traditional Chinese Medicine aspect, it improves the digestive system which also improves the complexion and gives the immune system a boost. These deeper benefits are outlined in different exercises within the book.*

Left: Pilates is a lifestyle, so the principles should be worked with every day in every situation.

CHI PILATES

ANATOMICAL TERMINOLOGY

During the book terminology is used to describe certain movements.

This is a quick check section for easy reference.

Flexion	This means whenever you are bending forward or sideways.
Extension	Is the opposite of flexion. This is when the body is lengthening (stretching), i.e. bending backward.
Abduction	When the arm or leg is taken out to the side away from the body.
Adduction	Opposite to abduction, i.e. bringing the leg back towards the body after lifting it out to the side.
Rotation	Turning round. Anatomically it means, movement around the axis of a bone.
Supine	Lying on your back.
Prone	Lying on your front.
Lateral	To the side.
Anterior	To the front.
Posterior	To the back.

Pilates is generally safe for anyone to do. However, should you have a medical condition, it is advisable to check with a Pilates practitioner or your doctor before you start.

There are some conditions where you need to avoid certain movements or positions as they may aggravate the condition

Did you know that four out of five adults living in the UK have had or will have back pain at some time or another in their lives? That's the bad news. The good news is if you have not suffered as yet with back pain you could keep it that way if you look after your posture now. Understanding how back pain starts in the first place can help you take the right steps to avoid it. Most articles on the subject go too deeply into the anatomical aspects and can confuse those who are not conversant with how the body works. This simple explanation using the analogy of the workplace may help you to understand how things can go terribly wrong in a short space of time.

Your spine and the muscles that support it work as a team. You have management (the spine), supervisors (your larger muscles) and the shop-floor workers (your smaller stabilising muscles). When everyone works together, you have a healthy workforce. If part of the team stops pulling their weight, through laziness or illness, the responsibility falls towards those working alongside. If the supervisors cannot sort the problem out, things will begin to escalate. The recruitment of an unqualified worker will be the first option. This will be acceptable for a while, but in time that worker will begin to complain. Management are normally the last to find out and when they do there is usually a lot of shouting to be heard.

STEPS TO A HEALTHIER BACK

If you have suffered with back problems, it is advisable for you to look carefully at your posture. Your pelvic alignment is the first port of call. To work with the positioning of the pelvis will immediately start the process of re-alignment in the spine. This is a preventative measure against back pain in the future. If you have structural curves in the spine, e.g. kyphosis/lordosis or scoliosis, locate a specialist to advise you on which muscle groups you need to stretch or strengthen in order to help stabilise your spine. An osteopath can help you with this.

If you have been given back exercises by a physiotherapist, following an accident or operation, look for a class locally when you have finished your treatment which focuses on stretching and strengthening the spine so you can continue with your programme. It is not advisable if you are suffering with back pain to engage in any weight-bearing exercises or high-impact aerobic exercise until you can stabilise the spine.

Below: if you have suffered with back problems, it is advisable for you to look carefully at your posture.

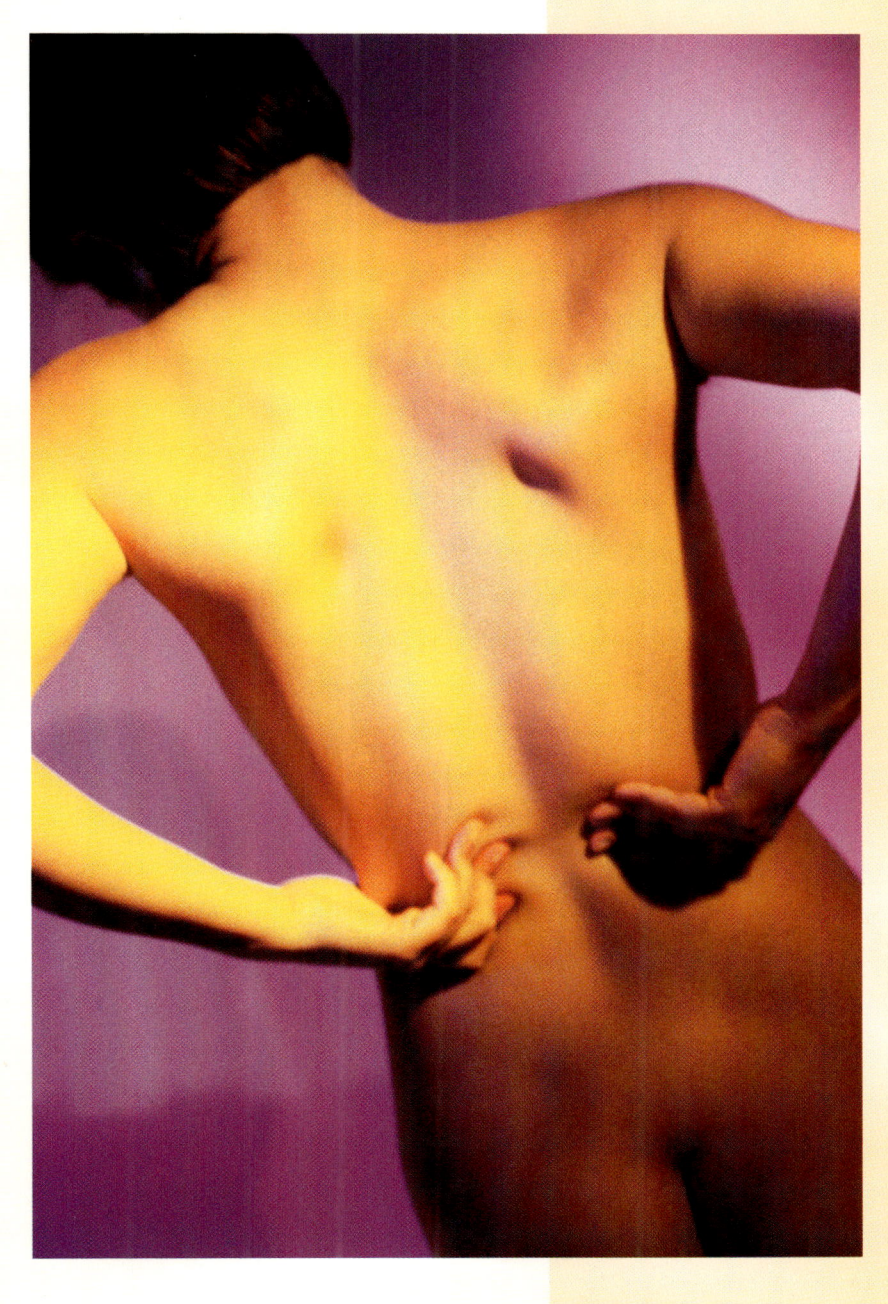

Right: the skeleton is the framework of the human anatomy, supporting the body and protecting its internal organs.

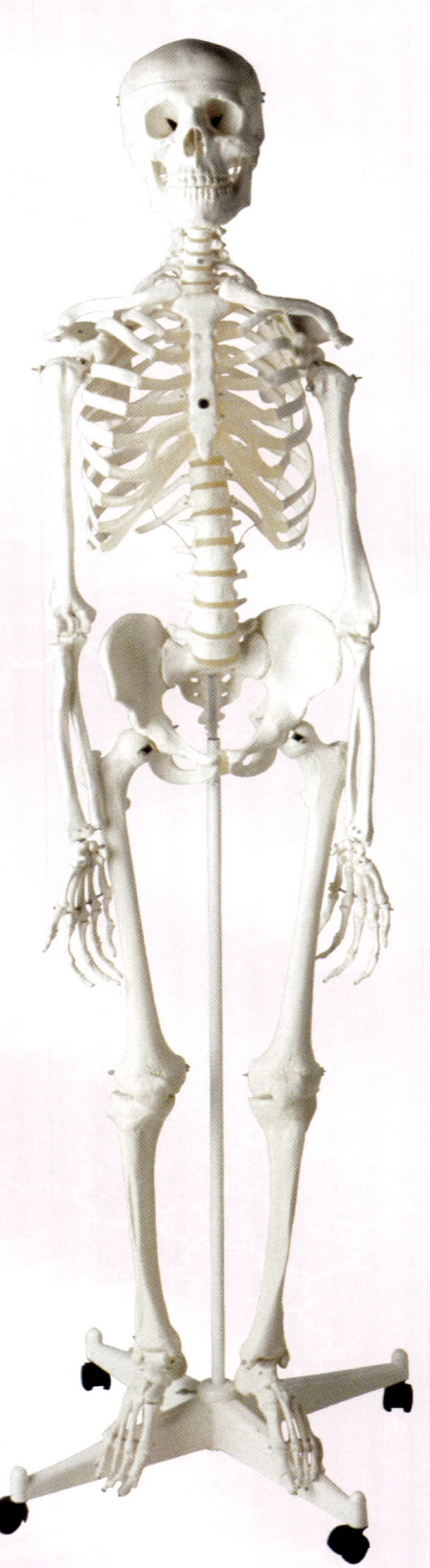

LOOKING AT POSTURE

Pilates once described the body as a finely tuned orchestra. When all sections work together, the result is perfect harmony.

Over the years our attention has been given to the outer muscles that we see in the mirror, and we attend classes for problem areas e.g. ' tums, bums, thighs'. 'bodytone' etc. In truth, the body is not made up of an outer and inner shell but is one whole, so we should work with it as such. You don't weed just half the garden or dust half a room. If you neglect one area, stagnant energy (weeds and dust) collects. Not only does this look untidy, it begins to effect everything around it.

The principles of Pilates are so logical that when you learn them you begin to wonder why you haven't followed them before. With modern technology we have become lazy in our movement patterns and, although we accept the fact that posture is important, we pay little attention to it. The skeleton is the framework of the human anatomy, supporting the body and protecting its internal organs. Two hundred and six bones make up the skeleton.

Male and female body structure is very similar; the exception being that female bones are usually lighter and thinner than those of the male. The spine and the ribs provide a

LOOKING AT POSTURE

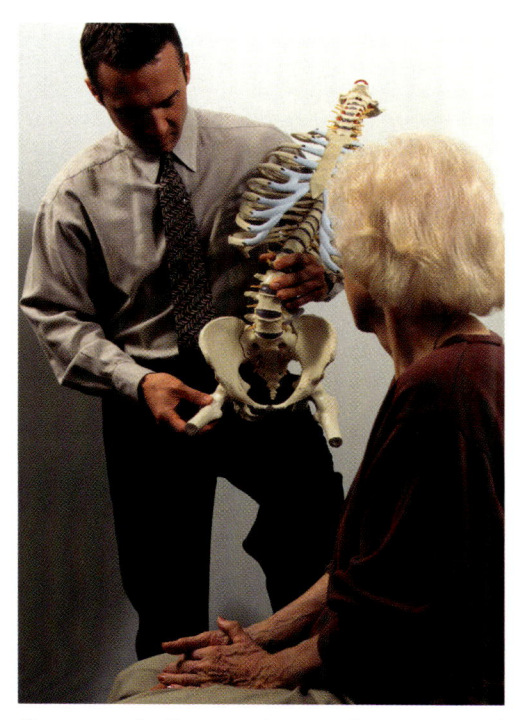

framework for our internal organs and it is therefore important that good alignment is kept, to allow sufficient room for these organs to function efficiently.

The spine is made up of 33 vertebrae. 7 cervical (in the neck) which is attached to the skull, 12 thoracic (where the ribs attach), 5 lumbar (lower back), 5 sacral (these are fused and form the sacrum) and 4 coccygeal (also fused to form the coccyx/tailbone).

The spinal cord is housed and protected by the spine, and conveys sensory messages from the brain to all parts of the body. Messages from the body to the brain are also transmitted back this way. If the vertebrae are put out of alignment, this displaces the discs sitting in between, causing them to either protrude posteriorly or anteriorly. Both conditions will irritate the spinal nerves, which will relay a message of discomfort to the brain.

The Chinese believe energy is transmitted through a similar network called meridian pathways. The energy within the body travels through these pathways freely if we have good posture. If we don't, then these messages have a more laboured journey and in some cases get lost along the way or are just blocked and cannot get through, causing that energy to stagnate. This they believe is the cause of discomfort and eventual pain. They also say that we start to receive these messages nine months before the onset of pain, but these signs on many occasions get ignored.

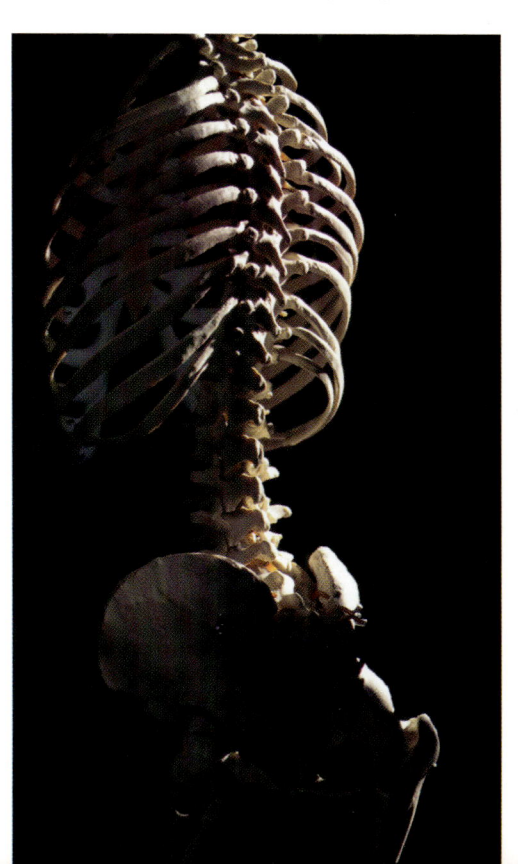

Left: the male and female body structure is very similar; the exception being that female bones are usually lighter and thinner than those of the male

Below: the spinal cord is housed and protected by the spine, and conveys sensory messages from the brain to all parts of the body.

LOOKING AT POSTURE

We are born with four natural curves in the spine – the cervical and lumbar curve and the thoracic and sacral curve. These curves, along with the intervertebral discs in between each vertebra, allow for cushioning and shock absorbency during movement. These curves also allow the spine to hold 10 times more weight than would be possible if it were straight. The main causes of back pain are down to poor posture, losing the natural curves because of faulty movement patterns, stress, decreased flexibility and poor physical fitness.

Our posture becomes habitual as we get older and, unless we are experiencing any pain or discomfort, we become oblivious to it.

The body is very clever at cheating. If a muscle is too weak to perform a movement, the body will recruit a larger, stronger muscle close by to assist. The result is the development of faulty movement patterns. The body will then send us a message informing us of this by means of a twinge or ache. How many times have we felt an ache but, because it doesn't leave us in a state of paralysis, we dismiss or ignore it, masking it with a painkiller, only to be reminded of it again the next day or next week a little more acutely?

These initial signs resemble a light tap on the door – if no one answers, the tap gets louder. This can go on until the tap increases to a loud knocking, which you cannot ignore any longer. Pilates helps us to become more aware of our body so we notice these early warning signs and take action a little earlier.

The normal curves of the spine can be seen in fig. A. A plumb line has been drawn down the centre of the body to show good alignment. The hip bones and the pubic bone are sitting vertically on the same plane. This indicates that the pelvis is in neutral. When the pelvis is in neutral, the lordotic curve is present. When the pelvis is not in neutral, the lordotic curve is lost or increased. If the hip bones are further forward than the pubic bone as in fig. B, the pelvis is in an anterior tilt and the lordotic curve is increased. If the hip bones sit further back than the pubic bone, this is a posterior tilt as in figs C and D and the lordotic curve is lost.

Aristotle was the first to describe and analyse the actions of muscles in the human body. He is referred to as the 'Father of Kinesiology'. It is your musculoskeletal system that allows your body to move.

Your muscles hold your skeleton in place. How you stand, sit or lie will depend on how you are using your muscles to do these activities. If you sit for prolonged periods, you will be overworking certain muscle groups at the expense

LOOKING AT POSTURE

of not working the opposing ones adequately and the results will be muscle imbalance. These imbalances affect the muscular, nervous and skeletal systems of the body.

There are around 600 muscles within the body. We have:

> **Skeletal** These are attached to the bones.
>
> **Smooth** These muscles are contained within the walls of the organs such as the stomach and intestines. We cannot control these muscles. They work involuntarily, e.g. to push food through the digestive system.
>
> **Cardiac** This muscle forms the wall of the heart and pumps the blood around the body.

The skeletal muscles are attached to the bones, which provide us with our voluntary movement patterns. They work with partners, i.e. the biceps and triceps are partners; the quadriceps and hamstrings are partners. When one muscle group contracts (shortens) it is called the concentric phase. When it lengthens, it is in the eccentric phase. While one muscle group is in the concentric phase, its partner is in the eccentric phase. In most conditioning programmes the emphasis is on the contraction, concentric, phase. In Pilates the emphasis is on the lengthening, eccentric, phase.

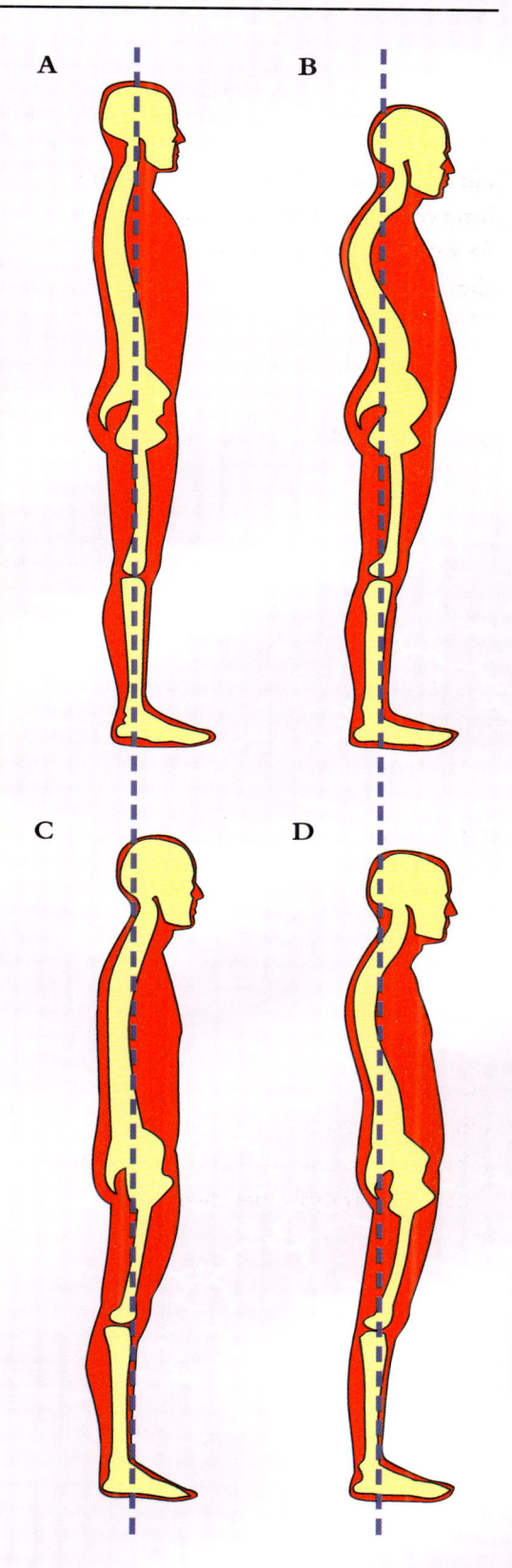

Left: four types of posture. Fig A, B, C and D

'LENGTHENING' AS OPPOSED TO STRETCHING

What can be misleading is the terminology of 'stretching' muscles. This can lead to people believing that they can make their muscles longer. Muscles cannot be stretched; they can only contract and when they contract they become shorter and then they lengthen again to their original length. Muscles shorten for a variety of reasons: bad posture, being tightened and overloaded during training, injury and illness. Short or tight muscles can be corrected by gently re-lengthening the fibres within the muscle, and this is what is commonly referred to as 'stretching'.

Below: unfortunately the majority of our daily activities lead us to bad posture.

If you try and stretch a muscle past its original length, you begin stretching the tendons or ligaments. Ligaments are like liquorice – once they are stretched they do not return to their original length. The elasticity of tendons is minimal. Tendons and ligaments assist in the stability of joints therefore if they are over-stretched the stability to some degree is lost.

The strength and length of our muscles, which support the skeleton, respond to our posture. Bad posture will result in certain muscles becoming either weak or short. Unfortunately the majority of our daily activities encourage bad posture. If we look at routine movements, we will see that the majority of activities are done with our arms forward of the body.

i.e. driving
washing up
typing
gardening
picking things up
cooking
sewing
D.I.Y.

How many activities can you think of that we can do with our arms behind us? Not a lot – that's why so many women can't do the zips up at the back of their dresses! That particular movement pattern is not regularly performed and the muscles are not adequately conditioned. Corrective exercises which focus on lengthening and conditioning underused muscles will immediately improve our posture and our health.

POSTURAL SCENARIO

Let's take the office worker who sits for prolonged periods and see where the common imbalances occur. Firstly, let's look at the muscles that are relaxing while sitting.

> *A. The buttocks*
> *B. Hamstrings*
> *C. Hip flexors*

The buttocks, hamstrings and hip flexors are all being supported by a chair. They are relaxing. The buttocks and quadriceps are in a lengthened position, but are becoming weak. The hamstrings are being kept in a shortened position, but they are also becoming weak because they are relaxing. The hip flexors are being kept short and will also weaken. When the person stands up those muscle groups will not support the skeleton correctly. Unless these muscles are conditioned accordingly, that person's posture will gradually deteriorate

Let's now look at the common torso position that usually accompanies a prolonged sitting posture.

When sitting, the requirements for strong abdominals and back muscles are significant to keep good alignment for a long period of time. As the muscles in the mid-back weaken and lengthen, the shoulder blades (scapulae) begin to drift away from the spine, allowing the shoulders to move forward. The weight of the shoulders is transmitted into the front of the body, into the breast bone (sternum). As the breast bone sinks, the ribs drop down, pulling the head forward. The head weighs between 10–15lb and that weight should be centrally balanced on top of the spine. The further forward it travels the heavier it becomes. This places a great deal of strain on the upper fibres of the trapezius muscle. This strain can lead to migraines, headaches and cervical strain. The weight of the head and torso is transmitted through the spine to the sacroiliac joint, which forms part of the pelvis. Any imbalance will effect the positioning of the pelvis, pulling it out of its neutral alignment.

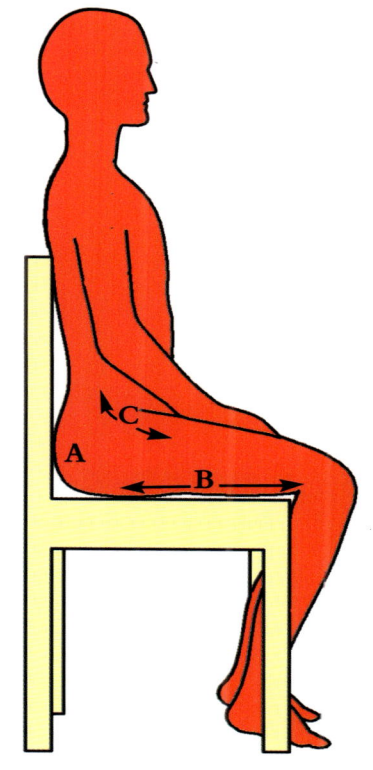

Left: the buttocks, hamstrings and hip flexors are all being supported by a chair.

POSTURAL SCENARIO

Owing to the chest becoming tighter, and the restriction of movement in the ribcage, the breathing is affected. Our lungs become less efficient, placing our immune system on alert.

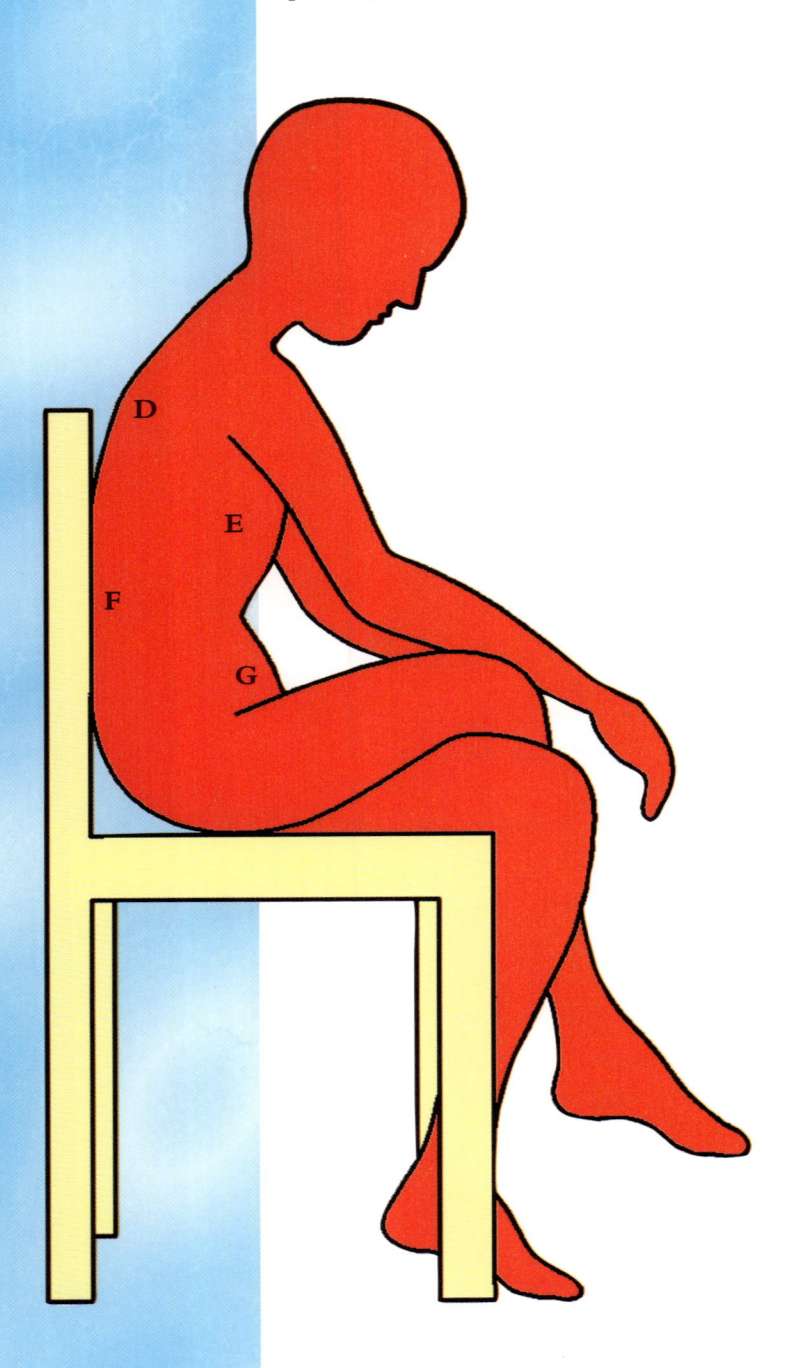

D. Trapezius
The trapezius is made up of three layers – the upper, middle and lower fibres. The upper fibres are overworked. The middle and lower fibres are underworked.

E. Pectoralis (chest)
The pectoralis (chest muscle) is being shortened.

F. Spine
The muscles supporting the whole spine are also overworking. It is important that the muscles, which support the spine, are equally balanced in strength and flexibility. Keeping them in this position weakens them.

G. Abdominals
The abdominals are relaxed, underworked and becoming weaker.

An example of some common physical problems caused by sitting for prolonged periods:

- *Tension in the upper back, shoulders and neck.*
- *Headaches, migraines.*
- *Chest complaints, colds, coughs, nasal congestion.*
- *Cold feet.*

Physiological symptoms:

- *Lack of self respect.*
- *Moodiness.*
- *Poor concentration.*
- *Selfishness.*

SELF-POSTURAL ANALYSIS

Follow these simple guidelines to check your own posture. To do this you need to see your figure so wear either tight clothing, e.g. a leotard, or be naked. Have access to a full-length mirror. Once you are aware of imbalances in the body, then you can choose the exercises that are going to help you correct them.

When you're ready, stand in front of the mirror with your eyes shut and stand normally. Don't adopt a posture that you think is correct because this will give you the wrong information about yourself. Open your eyes and start to view yourself from the feet upwards. During this don't alter your position. Fill out the self-postural analysis page in pencil so that you can go back to it in a couple of months' time.

Left: fill out the self-postural analysis in pencil so that you can go back to it in a couple of months' time.

```
         12
      9      3
         6
```

DATE _____

FEET *Standing within your clockface, where do your second toes point?*
KNEES ☐ normal ☐ knock-kneed ☐ bow-legged
☐ *further observations*
HIP BONES ☐ level ☐ right side higher ☐ left side higher
RIBCAGE ☐ level ☐ right side higher ☐ left side higher
☐ right/left side nearer to mid-line of body
SHOULDERS ☐ level ☐ right side higher ☐ left side higher
HEAD ☐ level ☐ tilted/shifted to right/left

Further observations if you have someone to help you.

View from the side in a standing position.
HEAD ☐ sitting neutral ☐ shifted forwards/back from shoulders
NECK ☐ short/long
UPPER BACK ☐ flat/rounded
LOWER BACK ☐ flat/over-arched
KNEES ☐ normal/hyperextended

View from the back
HEAD ☐ tilted/shifted to left/right
SHOULDERS ☐ level ☐ left/right higher
SHOULDER BLADES (SCAPULAE) ☐ level ☐ left/right higher
☐ left/right nearer to mid-line of body

Right: draw an imaginary line through the centre of your body and look at the position of your head in relation to the shoulders and the mid-line.

SELF-POSTURAL ANALYSIS

Questions to ask yourself as you go along:

- How are your feet placed? Are they parallel to one another? If you were standing on a clockface in the centre, where does your second toe point?

- How do your knees sit? Are they both pointing forward? Or are you knock-kneed? Bow-legged?

- Now you have to find your hip bones. Use your middle finger and do this with your eyes closed. Find the protruding bones of the hip and when you have found them keep your fingers there, open your eyes and check the level of your fingers. Are they level? Or is one finger higher than the other?

- Find your bottom rib in the same way as the hip bones. Again do this with the eyes closed then check the level of your fingers again. Are they level? Is one nearer to the mid-line of your body than the other?

- Look at your shoulders Are they level? Is one higher than the other?

- Draw an imaginary line through the centre of your body and look at the position of your head in relation to the shoulders and the mid-line. Is it sitting centrally on top of your shoulders? Is it sitting slightly to the left/right?

- When finding the shoulder blades, use the same technique as for the hip bones and ribcage.

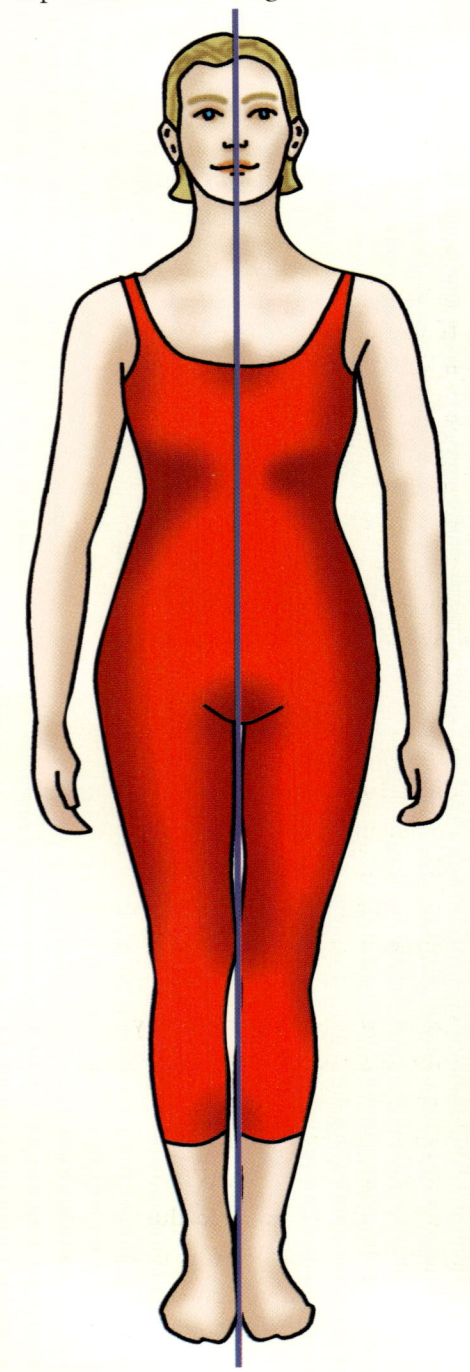

OSTEOPOROSIS AND PILATES

As we age, the rate of bone replacement gradually becomes slower and in extreme cases the result is osteoporosis. Osteoporotic bone becomes fragile and can fracture easily.

The density and strength of our bones is determined during our childhood. We finish growing in our early twenties. Once we stop growing, the density within our bones begins to deteriorate. The quality of our bones depends on our lifestyle, genetics, the exercise we do and the food we eat. As children the quality of those factors play a big part in our growth. If we have good healthy bones and have built a high density, then as we get older the rate at which our bones deteriorate will depend on how strong they were at the time we stopped growing. Once we stop growing, it is up to us to maintain the density we have by continuing to eat and exercise well.

If we look at the older generation we will see that as children they actually did a lot of exercise: they walked to and from school, they played in the playground and it was safe for them to play out at night. Consequently they were building good bone density.

Once you stop growing, you cannot increase the density any further. You have to maintain what you have by regular exercise and good diet including calcium. When you contract or lengthen a muscle during exercise it pulls on the bone it is attached to and this maintains the density. If you don't exercise, the bones begin to deteriorate. Osteoporosis has therefore kept its distance for some time in the older generation because their density was high to begin with.

A worrying factor is the more sedentary lifestyle we have today. How strong will our children's bones be in comparison to those of their grandparents when they stop growing? The positive side to this is it is never too late to maintain what you have and in Pilates the process of re-lengthening the muscles helps fight osteoporosis and helps to maintain bone density.'

Above: the density and strength of our bones is determined during our childhood.

CHI PILATES PRINCIPLES

The principles of Pilates are mapped out in five stages. These principles, if adhered to, can be used in your daily life. Learn them one at a time.

BREATHING

PELVIC ALIGNMENT AND STABILITY

RIBCAGE PLACEMENT

SCAPULAR PLACEMENT

CERVICAL PLACEMENT AND STABILITY

Below: it is never too late to maintain what you have with Pilates.

CHI PILATES PRINCIPLES

BREATHING

Breathing is like dancing. When we dance we use our feet, but there are various dances we could learn. When we breathe we use our lungs, but there are various breathing methods and Pilates breathing is just one.

The breath oxygenates the blood improving circulation. The blood and the food we eat also feed our internal organs. The quality of both should be equally important.

Many take their breathing for granted because the body breathes automatically. The way we breathe depends on our posture and mental state. If we feel anxious or stressed, our breathing becomes short and rapid and stays relatively up in the chest area. When we are relaxed and emotionally stable, our breathing is slower and deeper into the ribcage and abdomen.

Only when our breathing becomes laboured or stops, do we sit up and take notice. In the East breathing plays an important part in their philosophies because they believe that if you control your breath you control your life. In Pilates breathing also plays an important role.

Focusing on the breath automatically slows the breath rate down, relaxing the body, relaxing the muscles, relaxing the mind. Think how an athlete looks just before a race, focused but relaxed and ready to allow the body to perform effortlessly in the event it has been trained for.

The breathing for Pilates is called 'thoracic' breathing. It is not a deep breathing exercise – natural breathing is encouraged. Thoracic breathing means that we breathe into the thoracic area, into the ribcage. The ribcage goes all around the body so, as we breathe, we are attempting to expand the ribcage and work it like bellows.

Above: think how an athlete looks just before a race, focused but relaxed and ready to allow the body to perform effortlessly in the event it has been trained for.

CHI PILATES PRINCIPLES

Right: the mind has so many things to think about during the exercises that the breath is usually forgotten.

Mastering this breathing technique takes time. Most participants who start a Pilates programme will agree that the breathing is the most difficult part. The mind has so many things to think about during the exercises that the breath is usually forgotten. Although the exercises are executed with control, sometimes if you are challenged you will subconsciously hold your breath while consentrating on what you're trying to do. Remind yourself repeatedly to breathe naturally.

For the purpose of Pilates we breathe in through the nose and out through the mouth. When breathing in through the nose, the breath is taken into the lungs which helps to expand the ribcage giving room for the lungs to work efficiently. On the out-breath the breath comes from the abdominal cavity, encouraging the abdominals to contract which helps to stabilise the pelvis.

Anatomically, during exhalation muscles relax and movement can be executed more freely. The pattern of the breath during exhalation is that the ribs roll forward and the spine flexes, hence it is appropriate to do any flexion moves during exhalation. On inhalation the diaphragm moves down, allowing the ribs to expand, massaging the intercostal muscles. The spine during inhalation naturally extends; therefore it is logical to perform any extension exercise on the in-breath. An awareness of how the diaphragm moves during the in- and out-breath is cultivated during the exercises.

CHI PILATES PRINCIPLES

LEARNING TO BREATHE THORACICALLY

EXERCISE 1

- *Lie on your back with your knees bent. Place your hands on the abdomen and breathe in through the nose and take the breath down to the abdomen making the hands rise. As you breathe out through the mouth, feel the abdomen come down towards the spine and flatten out. Use a forceful out-breath to get the connection and awareness. Imagine you are blowing a paper boat across the top of a pond. Do this five to six times.*

- *Now place your hands on the upper part of the chest, just below the throat. Breathe in through the nose until your hands rise. On the out-breath feel the chest soften. Repeat this five to six times.*

- *Place one hand back on the abdomen and, as you breathe in, feel the chest rise then the abdomen. As you breathe out through the mouth, feel the abdomen fall and the chest soften. Repeat this five to six times.*

- *Now place your hands around your ribcage so the fingers touch one another. Breathe so that your fingers move apart and feel the ribs separating from one another. On the out-breath they should come back in towards one another again so that your fingers touch again. Do this five to six times. You are trying to take the ribs wide rather than allowing them to rise like the chest and abdomen. During this exercise, try to keep both the chest soft and the abdomen flat. This can take some time to master. Learning thoracic breathing is an exercise in itself.*

Learning the art of any breathing can change your life dramatically. Be prepared for all kinds of emotions to rise when you start doing this. You may feel frustrated by it, get angry or emotional. Whatever feelings come up, don't suppress them.

Below: lie on your back with your knees bent. Place your hands on the abdomen and breathe in through the nose and take the breath down to the abdomen making the hands rise.

CHI PILATES PRINCIPLES

EXERCISE 2

You will require a long scarf or band to place around the body. You can do this exercise kneeling, sitting or standing.

Taking the band around the body, cross it over at the front. Breathe into the ribcage and the hands holding the band will come closer together. During the out-breath, pull gently on the band to help close the ribcage. Try keeping the chest soft and abdomen flat. Also when breathing in keep the shoulders down.

> **Remember this is a natural breath pattern we are trying to achieve, not a deep breathing pattern.**

The following exercises are done lying on your back. As we go through the different principles you will learn postural awareness which will benefit your execution of the rest of the exercises in the book.

- *Lie on your back with your knees bent.*
- *Feet parallel and in line with your knees.*
- *Place a ball or rolled towel between your knees.*
- *Knees in line with your hip bones.*
- *Shoulders relaxed and down.*
- *Chin dropped slightly towards the chest.*

Right: taking the band around the body, cross it over at the front. Breathe into the ribcage and into the band, the hands will come closer together.

CHI PILATES PRINCIPLES

PELVIC ALIGNMENT AND STABILITY

The alignment of the pelvis plays an important role in the stability of the spine. The spine depends on the strength of the muscles that support the pelvis to give it its stability. These muscles are listed below:

Pelvic floor muscles
Transversus abdominis
Internal oblique
Multifidus

PELVIC FLOOR MUSCLES

To locate the pelvic floor muscles think of the muscles you pull up when you don't want to pass water. (If you have difficulty, try next time when you go to the toilet to stop in mid-flow.) In addition to these muscles helping to control urination, there is a muscular sling that supports and holds the bladder, bowel and uterus in place.

Next, think of the muscle you use when you don't want to pass wind. Don't clench the buttocks when doing this.

EXERCISE 1

- *Breathe in to the ribcage.*

- *During the out-breath draw the muscles up inside the body slowly and hold for a couple of seconds.*

- *Breathe in to slowly release them.*

- *Repeat 5–10 times.*

During Pilates you will be reminded to 'pull up' the pelvic floor muscles at the beginning of every out-breath. When this becomes familiar to you and the muscles become stronger, you will be able to hold the muscles up for more than one breath. However, the pelvic floor muscles need to be used regularly to maintain their strength. This exercise can be used on its own and can be done at any time whether you are sitting, standing, lying or working. 'Pull up' whenever you remember.

Above: to 'pull up' the pelvic floor muscles at the beginning of every out breath.

THE TRANSVERSUS ABDOMINIS

The abdominals are made up of four groups of muscles: the rectus abdominis; the external oblique, which are your outer sports muscles; the internal oblique; and the transversus abdominis (TA) which are your internal stabilising muscles.

The transversus abdominis gets its name because the fibres run across the body and form a band around the lumbar spine. The strength of those fibres will determine the stability of the lower spine. Regardless of how strong your sports muscles are, the internal stabilisers are the ones that stabilise the skeleton – if they are not strong then your stability is likely to be weak.

These internal muscles have been severely neglected until recently. In the past the focus was on external strength and little or no attention was paid to internal strength or stability. Pilates has brought the importance of internal strength to the attention of the fitness industry and it is now an integral part of all training programmes.

Locating these muscles can prove quite difficult initially. To get a feeling of what the internal stabilisers do, try this simple exercise.

Clasp your hands together and imagine your spine between your hands. Now squeeze the fingers into the back of the hands and also press the heel of the hands together. Now try and pull the fingers apart, keeping the heels of the hand together. That reaction is similar to when you contract the TA, pelvic floor, internal oblique and multifidus simultaneously.

Exercise 1
Visualisation (a)

Think of the muscle you pull in when zipping up a tight pair of trousers. That muscle is the TA.

- *Breathe in to the ribcage.*

- *Breathe out, 'pull up and in'.*

- *Breathe in to the ribcage and check the abdominals are still pulled in.*

- *Breathe out to pull up the pelvic floor again.*

- *Repeat 5–10 times.*

CHI PILATES PRINCIPLES

Left: internal muscles have been severely neglected until recently. Pilates has brought the importance of internal strength to the attention of the fitness industry and it is now an integral part of all training programmes.

Exercise 1
Visualisation (b)

Imagine you have a large belt wrapped around your body from the waist down to your hips and a strap which is attached to the front and back of the belt which goes between the legs. Now imagine the belt and strap is getting tighter

- *Breathe in to prepare.*

- *Breathe out and tighten the belt and strap.*

- *Breathe in to allow the strap to loosen, but the belt stays tight.*

- *Breathe out and tighten the strap again.*

The pelvic floor muscles will relax out, but you are aiming to keep the other muscles engaged for as long as possible. The longer you can keep them pulled, in the stronger they are becoming.

CHI PILATES PRINCIPLES

Above: the 'neutral' position of the pelvis means that the natural lordotic curve of the lumbar spine is present.

PELVIS PLACEMENT

Learning how your pelvis sits within your body is the first step to re-aligning any imbalances in the torso. There are two spinal positions to use when stabilising the pelvis, 'neutral spine' and 'imprinted spine'. The 'neutral' position of the pelvis means that the natural lordotic curve of the lumbar spine is present. The 'imprint' is when there is no lordotic curve.

Finding 'neutral' pelvis. Visualise the skeleton, and focus on the pelvis. Draw an imaginary line from one hip bone to the other then down to the pubic bone and back to the hip bone again and you will form the shape of a triangle. A neutral pelvis is when the three lines of the triangle sit on the same level.

The 'imprint' is when the pubic bone sits higher than the hip bones, flattening the back so it feels as if it were pressed gently down into the floor. If you were lying in putty, you would be 'imprinting' it.

EXERCISE 1
To find neutral and the imprint

Lie on your back with your knees bent. Place the heel of the hands on the hip bones, finger tips towards the pubic bone and thumbs towards your navel. This will form the shape of a triangle on the front of the body and is now covering the area of the pelvis.

Visualisation
Think of a clockface lying on the front of your body – 3 and 9 o'clock are your hip bones, 12 o'clock is the pubic bone and 6 o'clock is your navel. We are aiming for the clockface to be lying parallel to the floor.

- *Breathe in to the ribcage.*

- *Breathe out, 'pull up check abs' and tilt the pelvis, lifting 12 o'clock towards the ceiling, keeping the buttocks down. You are imprinting your spine into the floor.*

- *Breathe in to stay.*

- *Breathe out, 'pull up check abs' and tilt the pelvis so that 12 o'clock tilts down towards the floor. This position may feel awkward because you are pinching in the lower back. It is a position to avoid. We do not wish to over-arch the lordotic curve.*

- *Breathe in to stay.*

- *Breathe out to return to where you started.*

CHI PILATES PRINCIPLES

The neutral position is between the imprint and the over-arched position so the three bones are lying level and the clockface is parallel.

EXERCISE 2

As Exercise 1, only you stay in the neutral position throughout.

- *Breathe in to the ribcage.*

- *Breathe out to 'pull up and pull in'.*

- *Breathe in to the ribcage (keeping the abs pulled in).*

- *Breathe out to 'pull up' and check you are still pulled in. If you're not, this is the time to do it.*

Guidelines
- Don't imprint the spine when you are pulling up and in.
- Don't squeeze the buttocks.

Repeat this 8–10 times.

The difference between neutral pelvis and neutral spine

When lying on your back (supine) with the head on the floor, the skeleton has its natural cervical and lordotic curves present therefore it is in a neutral position. The pelvis is also in neutral

When flexing the upper body off the floor, the neutral spine has been lost but the pelvis is still in neutral, so you have neutral pelvis but not neutral spine.

Exercises in the supine position with one or both feet on the floor are generally performed with a neutral pelvis.

Exercises in the supine position with both feet off the floor are generally performed in the imprint until you have strengthened the stabilisers to hold neutral.

There are exceptions to this and guidelines will be set out for each exercise.

Below: when lying on your back (supine) with the head on the floor, the skeleton has its natural cervical and lordotic curves present therefore it is in a neutral position. The pelvis is also in neutral.

CHI PILATES PRINCIPLES

RIBCAGE PLACEMENT

Your ribs surround your body and attached to the ribs are the abdominals.

As you lie on the floor, become familiar with the lowest rib in your back. This rib should be touching the floor. It remains on the floor throughout. If it rises, you have lost your stability.

EXERCISE 1

- *Breathe in to the ribcage.*
- *Breathe out, 'pull up check abs', allow the ribs to slide down towards the hips.*
- *Repeat 5–10 times.*

SCAPULAR MOVEMENT

The scapulae (shoulder blades) are the only bones in your body not attached to another bone. They have a great deal of mobility and can move upward, downward, inward, outward and rotate. To stabilise the scapulae in the back, aim to keep them wide and down especially during arm movement. There should be a feeling of gently sliding the scapulae down the back, without forcing them.

Below: as you lie on the floor, become familiar with the lowest rib in your back. This rib should be touching the floor. It remains on the floor throughout. If it rises, you have lost your stability.

CHI PILATES PRINCIPLES

Exercise 1

- *Breathe in to the ribcage.*

- *Breathe out, pull up and in and raise the arms towards the ceiling.*

- *Breathe in and reach further to the ceiling, allowing the shoulder blades to move away from the spine.*

- *Breathe out to bring the shoulders back down (keep the arms straight and fingers pointing to the ceiling). The shoulder blades come back towards the spine.*

- *Breathe in to reach to the ceiling.*

- *Breathe out to bring the shoulders back down.*

- *Repeat 5–10 times.*

Plus the following observations.
Try to take your mind away from the arms and focus on the shoulder blades.

Bring both arms down by your side. Keep them there while you breathe into the ribcage and feel the shoulder blades go wide in your back along the floor away from the spine.

Breathe out, pull up and in and feel your shoulder blades come closer together without pinching.

Repeat 5–10 times.

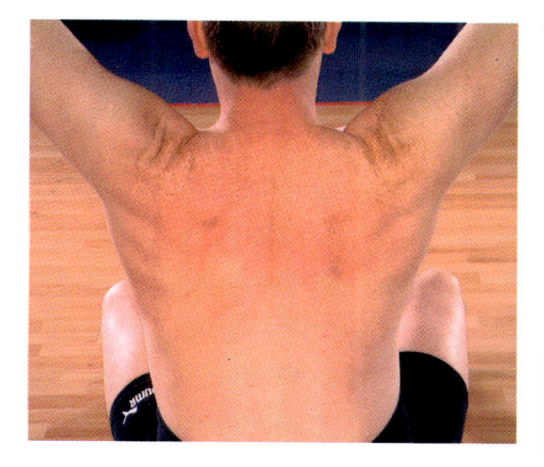

Stay lying on your back, breathe in to the ribcage and shrug the shoulders towards the ears. Breathe out to move the shoulders back down.

Again, forget the arm movement and think of this move coming from the shoulder blades.

Repeat 5–10 times.

The feeling of sliding the shoulder blades down is the engaging of the shoulder stabilising muscles in the back. This position is the postural stabilising position for the shoulder blades when executing a move.

Exercise 2

- *Breathe in to the ribcage and feel the shoulder blades going wide across the back.*

- *Breathe out through the mouth, pull up and in, slide the ribcage down and feel the shoulder blades come back.*

- *Repeat 5–10 times.*

Left: this shows the position the shoulder blades should be in when doing this exercise, but you should be in the lying position.

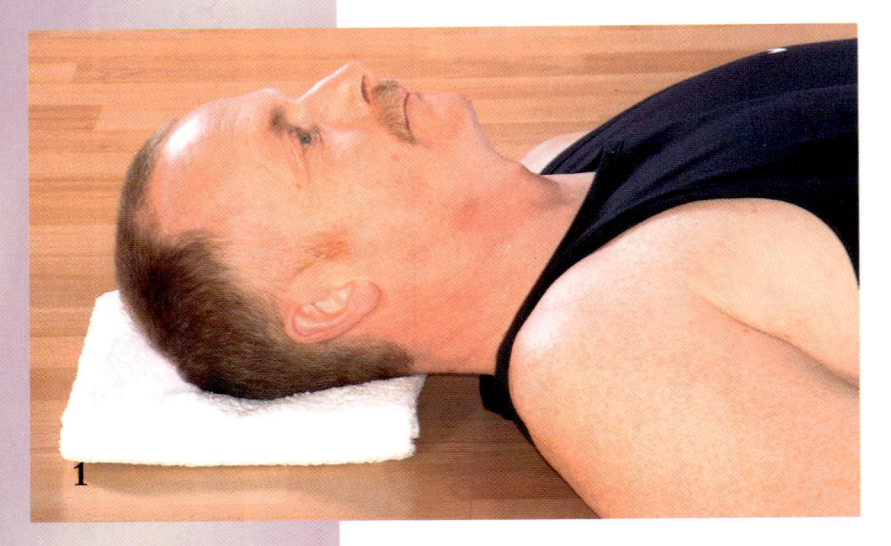

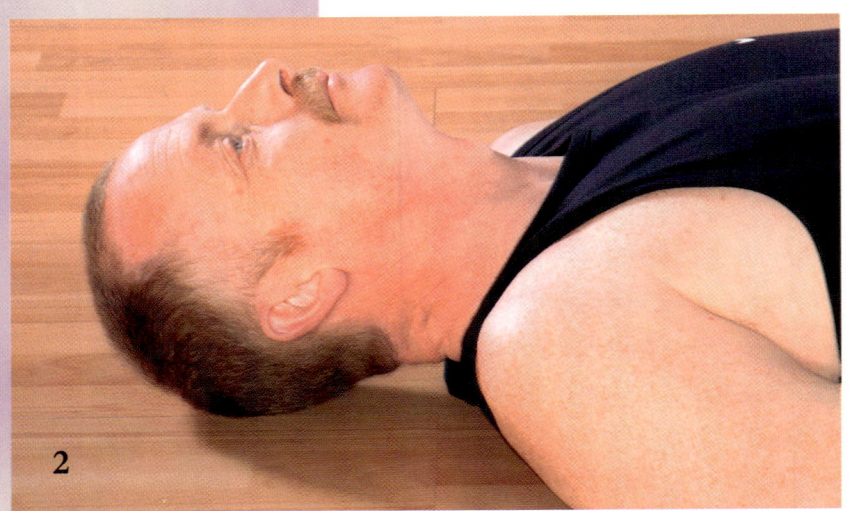

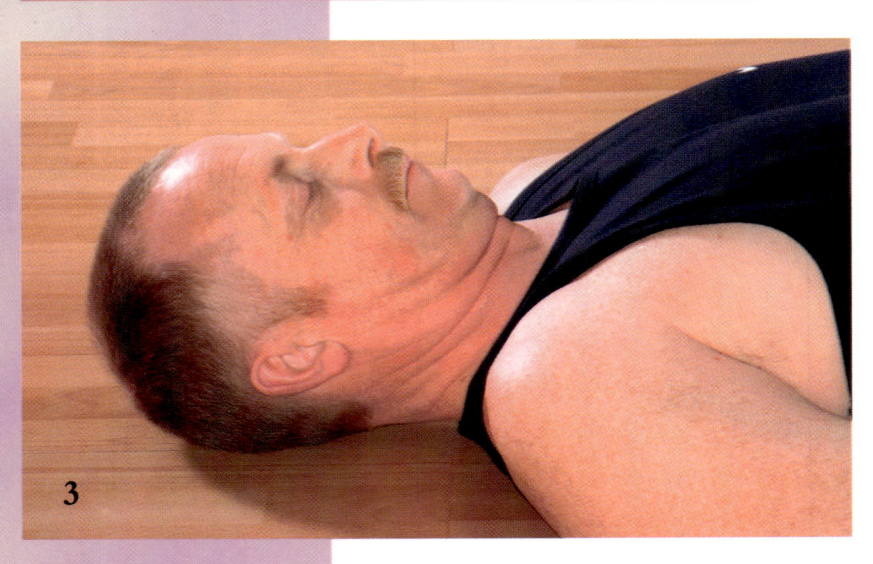

HEAD AND CERVICAL SPINE PLACEMENT

The head should sit centrally on top of the shoulders. The relationship between the head and shoulders should remain the same, no matter what position the rest of the body is in, whether you are standing, sitting, lying supine or prone (1).

Care should be taken when lifting the head off the floor from a supine position. The neck muscles are conditioned to carry the weight of the head when upright. When lying down, the head is usually supported by other means and the neck muscles can relax. Consequently, when they are asked to lift the head from a supine position, they are not conditioned and straining can occur

   1 – correct posion
   2 and 3 – incorrect positions

EXERCISE 1

- *Breathe in to the ribcage and drop the chin slightly towards the chest (try placing a piece of paper under the head then ask someone to slide the paper away). It is a subtle movement of dropping the chin and lengthening the neck without jamming the chin to the chest, (3).*

- *Breathe out. Pull up and in.*

- *Repeat 5–10 times.*

CHI PILATES PRINCIPLES

Exercise 2

- *Breathe in to the ribcage and lengthen the neck.*
- *Breathe out.*
- *Pull up the pelvic floor muscles.*
- *Pull in the abdominals.*
- *Slide the ribcage down.*
- *Keep the shoulder blades wide and relaxed.*
- *Repeat 5–10 times.*

The five basic Chi Pilates principles aim to rebalance and re-align the muscles that support the skeleton.

When this happens, flexibility and mobility within the joints become freer and more fluid with less tension. We all want to be able to do the things that our spine is capable of: to bend forwards, backwards, sideways and to be able to turn around without fear of straining or putting our back out.

Use the five principles to build up awareness of your body and try to incorporate them into your daily life. If, when you put this book down, you think about your posture once more than you did before you picked it up, you have stepped onto the pathway that will lead you to a better posture, stronger back, flatter abdominals, longer leaner muscles and a great sense of achievement.

Far left: position 1 - Breathe in to the ribcage and drop the chin slightly towards the chest. Positions 2 and 3 are incorrect.

Below: Pilates can lead to a better posture, stronger back, flatter abdominals, longer leaner muscles and a great sense of achievement.

Below: standing – weight equally distributed between both feet and between the balls of the feet, and heels.

POSTURAL POSITIONS

Whatever position you are in posture is important. These instructions apply whatever you are doing. You are attempting to keep the posture of your body in good alignment while performing these exercises, and also in your daily life.

STANDING

When standing:

- *Feet parallel.*

- *Weight equally distributed between both feet and between the balls of the feet and heels.*

- *Knees in line with the feet.*

- *Hips level and the pelvis in neutral.*

- *Abdominals pulled in*

- *Ribcage down.*

- *Shoulder blades wide and down the back.*

- *Neck long and relaxed*

- *Head sitting centrally on top of the shoulders.*

POSTURAL POSITIONS   37

SITTING

- *Feet parallel. Weight between the ball and heel of the foot.*

- *Knees in line with the feet and the hip bones.*

- *Pelvis in neutral.*

- *Abdominals pulled in.*

- *Spine in neutral.*

- *Neck long and relaxed.*

- *Head balanced centrally on top of the shoulders.*

SIDE-LYING

- *Feet parallel, one resting on top of the other.*

- *Knees in line.*

- *Pelvis in neutral.*

- *Abdominals pulled in.*

- *Waist (oblique muscle) lifted to support internal organs.*

- *Ribcage down.*

- *Shoulder blades wide and relaxed.*

- *Shoulders aligned.*

- *Lower arm supporting the head Head sitting centrally on top of the shoulders.*

- *Top arm resting in front for stability.*

Above: feet should be parallel, one resting on top of the other when side-lying.

Far left: sitting — knees in line with the feet and the hip bones.

POSTURAL POSITIONS

Above: knees should be bent and in line with the feet and hip bones when lying supine.

Below: back of the knees should be in line with the heels and sit-bones when lying prone.

LYING SUPINE

- Feet parallel.
- Knees bent and in line with feet and hip bones.
- Pelvis in neutral.
- Abdominals pulled in.
- Ribcage down.
- Shoulder blades wide and relaxed.
- Neck long and relaxed.
- Head sitting centrally on top of the shoulders.

LYING PRONE

- Feet parallel.
- Back of knees in line with the heels and sit-bones.
- Pelvis in neutral.
- Abdominals pulled in.
- Ribcage down.
- Shoulder blades wide and down in the back.
- Arms lifted off the floor parallel to the body.
- Head lifted and sitting centrally on top of the shoulders.

POSTURAL POSITIONS

ON ALL FOURS

- Feet parallel.

- Knees apart in line with feet and directly under the hips.

- Pelvis in neutral.

- Abdominals pulled up.

- Ribcage and shoulder blades down.

- Head up and placed centrally on the top of the shoulders.

- Arms straight and directly under the shoulders.

Above: knees should be apart in line with the feet and directly under the hips when on all fours.

40

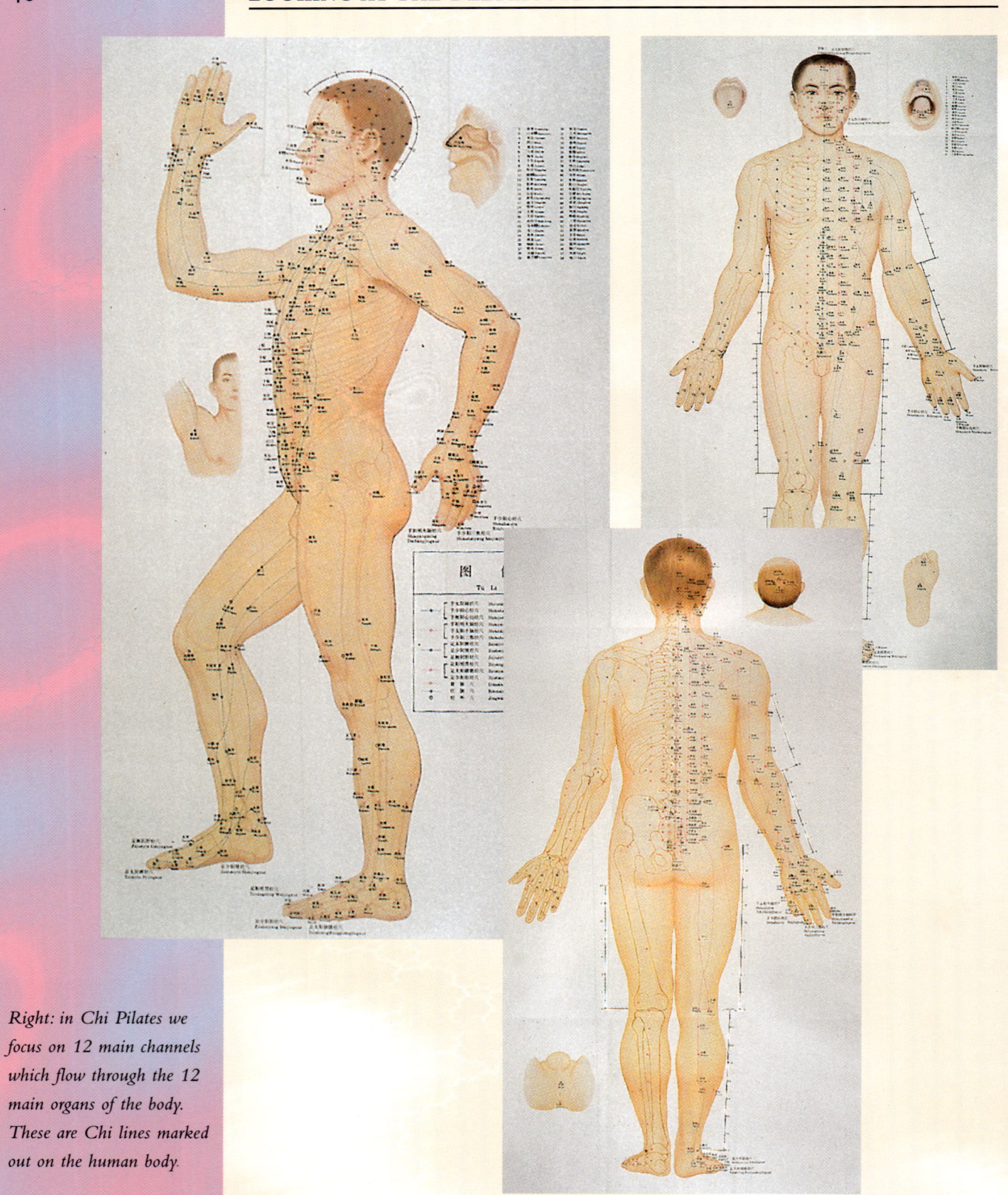

LOOKING AT THE DEEPER PICTURE – EAST AND WEST RE-UNITED

Right: in Chi Pilates we focus on 12 main channels which flow through the 12 main organs of the body. These are Chi lines marked out on the human body.

LOOKING AT THE DEEPER PICTURE – EAST AND WEST RE-UNITED

For thousands of years the Chinese have passed traditions down through the family relating to their health and spirituality. Their objective is to live long and stay healthy and, until recently, doctors in China were only paid if their patients were well. Eastern traditions are now becoming more widely accepted and many people seeking answers to questions that have eluded Western medicine in the past are turning to those who practise traditional remedies.

Below: Chinese traditions relating to health and spirituality have been passed down through the family.

Oriental medicine works with the energy of nature. Energy is all around us and within us. The energy within the body is similar to an electric circuit board. The channels of energy travel up and down the body. At certain points on the body this energy can be accessed to free it up from blockage or to stimulate it. These are the points used in Shiatsu and acupuncture. The channels through which the energy flows are sometimes referred to as meridians. There are hundreds of meridian pathways, but for the purpose of the exercises in Chi Pilates we are focusing on 12 main channels, which flow through the 12 main organs of the body.

The philosophy of oriental medicine is that a healthy mind results in a healthy body.

LOOKING AT THE DEEPER PICTURE – EAST AND WEST RE-UNITED

Chi Pilates works with five principles, Traditional Chinese Medicine works with five elements.

WOOD	Breath
FIRE	Alignment
EARTH	Stability
METAL	Focus
WATER	Relaxation

The elements are closely associated with the 12 main internal organs of the body.

WOOD	Liver/gallbladder
FIRE	Heart/small intestine Secondary organs Pericardium and triple heater
EARTH	Stomach/spleen
METAL	Lung/large intestine
WATER	Kidney/bladder

In Chi Pilates exercises we are helping to open up the channels by lengthening the muscles.

The energy (chi) running within the body will flow freely if the body is in good alignment. If not, then the energy gets stuck and begins to stagnate. The corresponding organ of whichever channel energy is prevented from flowing through will, in time, be affected by lack of energy.

Mind, body and spirit are all affected by change whether it be internal, for example, posture, injury, illness or diet, or external, for example environmental change i.e. weather, atmosphere or temperature. Any change will directly affect the energy around and within us, including our psychological and physiological state.

There are deeper issues involved, which are outside the remit of this book, but I hope I have included enough information for you to appreciate the wider picture.

LOOKING AT THE DEEPER PICTURE – EAST AND WEST RE-UNITED

Below: The Five Element Cycle.

FIRE SUMMER RED
Heart – Small Intestine
Pericardium – Triple heater
Late morning/Early afternoon
Tongue – Taste

EARTH LATE SUMMER YELLOW
Stomach – Spleen
Afternoon/Early evening
Mouth – Taste

WOOD SPRING GREEN
Liver – Gallbladder
Early/Late morning
Eyes – Sight

METAL AUTUMN WHITE
Lung – Large Intestine
Evening
Nose – Smell

WATER WINTER BLUE
Kidney – Bladder
Night
Ears – Hearing

LOOKING AT THE DEEPER PICTURE – EAST AND WEST RE-UNITED

WOOD: LIVER/GALLBLADDER

Wood is the element of spring. The colour associated with wood is green. It represents everything that grows upwards in the literal and metaphorical sense. The time of day for the wood element begins at dawn, the start of the day, as spring is the start of the year. Wood also represents birth and growth. Every action we do is the result of a single thought. The fruition of that thought depends on the strength of our wood element. The initial thought comes from the

Below: wood is the element of spring. The colour associated with wood is green.

water element, which precedes wood. We look at water in detail later because it is the last element but, because water gives birth to wood, it is also present at the beginning. The creative phase of any project is represented by wood which influences our decisions and helps us to see our way forward. Consequently if the wood element in our body is stagnant, our thinking will be indecisive, our eyesight affected and our creativity slow. This can result in emotional consequences which lead to frustration, irritability and lack of direction. If, however, our wood element is strong then our focus is clear, we see our projects through and we realise our dreams, because wood gives us the power to see our thoughts and plans come to fruition.

Each element represents a part of the body and wood represents the muscles, joints, ligaments and tendons. The organs associated with wood are the liver and gallbladder. The function of the liver and gallbladder in oriental medicine is to ensure the flow of energy (chi). to the muscles, joints, ligaments and tendons. Part of the liver's job is to store blood which is then used to feed those areas during physical activity. Part of the gallbladder's job is to ensure the energy is delivered. Quality blood results in quality performance. Your diet and the air you breathe determine the quality of your blood and therefore your well-being.

If energy is not getting through adequately, the result is an imbalance of that element. An element can be unbalanced at both ends of the scale. Too much energy being delivered can be as dangerous as too little.

LOOKING AT THE DEEPER PICTURE – EAST AND WEST RE-UNITED

An imbalance of the liver/gallbladder could be indicated by:

- *Muscle weakness (often seen in cases of multiple sclerosis).*
- *Visual weakness – yellow tinge or dryness in the eyes.*
- *Dizziness.*
- *Skin discoloration (as seen in jaundice).*
- *Brittle or discoloured nails.*
- *Low blood pressure.*
- *Indecision – inability to make your mind up*
- *Dreaming, never doing. Difficulty with bending or stretching.*
- *Shortness of breath.*
- *Menstrual cramps.*
- *Anger – irritability.*
- *Lack of energy.*
- *Over-planning but not achieving.*

When there is an imbalance in one element it will eventually effect the next element in the cycle. As the elements evolve, if there is a deficiency in one it will either draw energy from the one before or the one ahead, causing their energy levels to become weaker.

Exercises for the wood element – liver and gallbladder

Keeping in tune with nature, these exercises are best performed in the morning when the wood element is strongest. Ideally they are best performed outside, preferably close to any woody plant or tree. In the East the morning is when they do their T'ai Chi. At the break of dawn in the parks you will find hundreds of people taking their morning exercise together before they start their day.

Exercises for the liver/gallbladder:

Balance	Ankle circles
Seated twist	Warm-up
Shoulder bridge	Oblique
Side-lying hip extension	
Hip roll	Lizard
Arm circles	Press-ups

LOOKING AT THE DEEPER PICTURE – EAST AND WEST RE-UNITED

FIRE – HEART AND SMALL INTESTINE

SECONDARY ORGANS – PERICARDIUM AND TRIPLE HEATER

Fire is the element of summer. It is born out of wood so is the child of wood. It represents the peak of everything – the highest position, the ultimate goal, the finishing line, a time for celebration.

Below: fire is the element of summer. It is born out of wood so is the child of wood.

Think of a colour that would represent fire and you would probably come up with the colour red. The time of day for fire is high noon, mid-day, and it is at this time that our energy is at its highest. We are more productive and creative during mid-day hours. The heart, which governs the blood, pumping it around the body, is affected by the fire element. The heart has the greatest influence on the mind and on conscious thought. The heart is the organ most vulnerable to our emotions. If we open up our heart, we allow the possibility for others to come in and either help us or destroy us.

Below are common expressions we use, relating to the heart:

I didn't have the heart to tell them.
My heart bleeds for you.
She put her heart and soul into it.
We describe people as 'cold-hearted' or 'warm-hearted'.

If we have excess heart energy, the result will be a build-up of heat within the body and will show up as redness in the face, nervous laughter or anxiety. If there is deficiency in the heart energy, this will show as restlessness, fidgety hands and an inability to follow things through to the end. Eyes will be dull which reflect a lack of energy within the heart.

The small intestine receives food from the stomach where its job is to take out the nutrients and get rid of the waste.

When the foetus is developing, the heart develops first and the spleen second. This is why they are coupled together because they work together to feed the body and rid it of its waste. If the small intestine is weighed down with toxins or fatty foods then the process will slow down as the

LOOKING AT THE DEEPER PICTURE – EAST AND WEST RE-UNITED

lining of the intestine wall gets blocked and the nutrients can't get through. The consequences of nutrients not being absorbed efficiently will show up on the body's surface, as skin allergies or complaints. Dry skin is also a common symptom of spleen deficiency.

The two secondary organs associated with fire are the pericardium (also known as the heart protector) and the triple heater. The pericardium surrounds and protects the heart. Eastern philosophies state that its function is also to protect the heart against emotional trauma.

The triple heater is the only non-physical organ. It regulates the heat in the body, acting as our internal thermostat. A weakness in the energy of the triple heater would be indicated if the person was very sensitive to changes of temperature externally and internally.

Our sense of taste is also linked to fire because the heart supplies the tongue with large amounts of blood. Should there be imbalance in the heart channel, your sense of taste would change.

Exercises for the heart/small intestine:

Balance	Forward roll
Ankle circles	Knee lifts
Warm-up	100
Shoulder bridge	Single leg
Double leg	Breast stroke
Rocking	Press-ups
Arm circles	

Pericardium/triple heater:

Balance	Warm-up
Arm circles	Inner thighs
Table balance	

Below: arm circles exercise

LOOKING AT THE DEEPER PICTURE – EAST AND WEST RE-UNITED

EARTH – Stomach/spleen

The earth element has a strong connection to Chi Pilates because the majority of the exercises are performed on the floor, close to earth. Earth is at the centre of the Five Element Cycle and is therefore considered the stabilising force for the other four.

The season for earth is late summer. In oriental medicine there are five seasons.

Spring	Wood
Summer	Fire
Late summer	Earth
Autumn	Metal
Winter	Water

Earth is the child of fire, but is the mother of all the other elements. This element is also known as soil. The soil collects nutrients and moisture from the atmosphere, from growing plants and trees and from the decomposition of dead leaves, animals and plants. This transitional period between death and new birth gives us our ingredients for life. Our food, air and water all come from Mother Earth.

The earth supports us, so everything potentially that can support, surround or contain is represented by earth. A house, a chair, a bottle, a nest, a bath, our body – they are all 'earth' elements. In exercise Pilates brings us down to earth. It supports us while we execute certain movements and makes us feel safe.

The internal organs connected to earth are the stomach and spleen. These are our nurturing organs through which we digest and eliminate the food we eat, maintaining the nutrients, getting rid of the waste. The stomach sends food down to the small intestine and spleen.

If the pathways down are blocked, the waste products are sent back up in the form of belching, hiccups or, more severely, vomiting. Once the spleen receives food from the stomach, it extracts the goodness and energy then distributes it throughout the body via the blood vessels.

Our food is our medicine. We can nurture or abuse our body by what we put into it. Eating while stressed does not induce good digestion, nor does eating while distracted as the blood allocated for digestion is diverted to the brain. Therefore watching television while eating causes disharmony in the digestive process. 'Eating on the run' also has

Below: earth is at the centre of the Five Element Cycle and is therefore considered the stabilising force for the other four.

LOOKING AT THE DEEPER PICTURE – EAST AND WEST RE-UNITED

grim consequences if done regularly. The food you eat is first passed into the mouth through the lips. The lips, mouth and throat are all affected if the energy within the stomach or spleen is deficient or in excess.

Disharmony within the stomach/spleen can show up as these symptoms:

- Poor appetite, poor digestion.
- Obesity, abdominal distension.
- Heartburn.
- Belching.
- Cold sores.
- Coated tongue.
- Bruising easily.
- Prolapse.
- Poor concentration.
- Lack of energy.
- Nosebleeds.
- Spinal pain.
- Tired, heavy legs.

Psychological symptoms:

- Feeling unable to achieve.
- Selfishness.
- Excessive worrying.
- Frustration with life.

Exercises for the stomach/spleen:

Balance	Warm-up
Roll-up	Single leg
Oblique	Double leg
Side-lying hip extension	
Roll-down	Breast stroke
Table balance	Swan dive

Below: single leg exercise

LOOKING AT THE DEEPER PICTURE – EAST AND WEST RE-UNITED

METAL – Lungs/Large Intestine

Above: metal is related to the evening phase of the day when things should be quietening down.

Metal is the element of autumn. It is the child of earth. Born deep inside the earth, minerals and ores form crystals and precious stones which are symbolic of this element. It is related with the evening phase of the day when things should be quietening down. During the autumn nature prepares for the longer, darker, colder days and nights ahead. Metal energy in the body will utilise the nutrients gathered during the previous seasons to use as defences against the changes in climate.

The organs associated with metal are the lungs and large intestine. Deciding what is useful and what is not is attributable to metal and its related organs. The strength of metal energy assists our ability to know what is right from wrong, giving us our sense of judgement, to be able to see our way clearly and decisively.
Metal energy helps us in our ability to 'let go' of emotional baggage and show our feelings openly. Deficient energy will make us shy away from all emotions including joy, laughter and love, making us seem unapproachable, stand-offish and abrupt, often accompanied by depression, being withdrawn and 'blinkered'. The nose is the sense organ related to metal; the lungs and large intestine therefore govern our sense of smell. The expression to 'follow your nose' is to use your instinctive judgement, which you will do successfully if your energy is strong, unsuccessfully if your energy is weak.

Should the air we breathe contain pollutants, hair follicles in the nose will attempt to stop them before they enter the lungs. Our defensive system is besieged by these pollutants trying to enter the body every day. When we ingest food and drink the digestive system, which includes the large intestine, filters out what is good and bad. The quality of the food, drink and air we ingest will dictate the quantity of energy that is then transmitted around the body by the blood.

Our immune system, which protects us against infection and disease, acquires its strength from the energy supplied by these organs. Owing to the invasion from environmental poisons, the immune system is overwhelmed and its strength and

LOOKING AT THE DEEPER PICTURE – EAST AND WEST RE-UNITED

efficiency is challenged regularly. The energy in the lungs and large intestine, therefore, is invaluable to our health and well-being as any dysfunction in either will greatly affect our ability to fight off infection and disease. If this is coupled with the energy channels being blocked through bad posture, the risk of infection is increased dramatically.

Deficiency in metal – lungs/large intestine:

- Lung congestion.
- Susceptibility to colds and flu.
- Shortness of breath.
- Coughing.
- Dry skin.
- Skin complaints.
- Constipation.
- Poor circulation.
- Difficulty raising arms.
- Inability to grieve.
- Destructive towards oneself.
- Neurotic.
- Judgmental towards others.

Exercises for the lungs/large intestine:

Balance	Ankle circles
Warm-up	100
Roll-up	Leg circles
Double leg	Breast stroke
Arm circles	Swan dive
Press-ups	

Below: swan dive exercise.

LOOKING AT THE DEEPER PICTURE – EAST AND WEST RE-UNITED

WATER – BLADDER/KIDNEYS

Water is the element of winter. It represents our ability to survive. It is the creator of all things, but it also represents finality. At the conclusion of anything there is a transitional period of rest and recovery, where energy can re-charge before starting again. During this period we fall into an unknown void.

Certain animals fall into this abyss during the winter when they hibernate. Humans enter it at night when they sleep.

The unknown often gives rise to the emotion of fear. We experience this feeling of anxiety when we approach a situation we are uncertain of. Once we have approached and surmounted our fear, we very often wonder what caused us to worry in the first place. The initial fear will make us step forward or it may make us step back into the comfort of what we already know. This can make us shallow in our approach and our energy can stagnate. If we move forward and face our fear, we acquire knowledge, more understanding and wisdom.

Looking at how the cycle evolves, you will see what goes around comes around. Nothing stands still.

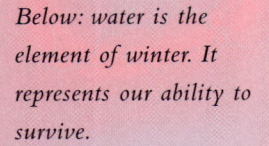

Below: water is the element of winter. It represents our ability to survive.

Taking an average of 100 years' life span, our element cycle evolves thus:

Wood	morning	spring	birth – 25yrs
Fire	mid-day	summer	birth 25 – 40yrs
Earth	late afternoon	late summer	40 – 70yrs
Metal	evening	autumn	70 – 100yrs
Water	night	winter	death – re-birth.

LOOKING AT THE DEEPER PICTURE – EAST AND WEST RE-UNITED

While we sleep the body heals itself and restores its energy. During the winter the hours of darkness are longer. We know instinctively that we should rest for longer periods during these months, but we fight it off because we are not conditioned to go with the flow and to listen to our body.

Our schedule during the winter is very often the same as in the summer. We work the same hours, do the same activities, eat the same foods and rest for the same periods of time. We are able to do this because we have electricity to provide light. Our supply of food comes from all over the world so we are not restricted anymore to the foods that grow specifically for us during winter. Our workload is greater than ever all through the year and we are able to communicate with everyone at anytime. One hundred years ago the amount of information available within one year is now equivalent to the amount of information we receive every day. Is it any wonder stress levels are high? But how many of us take steps to counterbalance this with relaxation.

If you are on the go all day, in the evening your activities should be of a more relaxing nature such as Chi Pilates or yoga. If your job involves you sitting during the day then some form of aerobic exercise should be done after work, followed by some strengthening exercises for the muscles that have been relaxing in your workchair all day. Those who do balance their activities proclaim profound improvements in their health and well-being.

Above: our schedule during the winter is very often the same as in the summer. We work the same hours, do the same activities, eat the same foods and rest for the same periods of time.

LOOKING AT THE DEEPER PICTURE – EAST AND WEST RE-UNITED

An example of how we do not work with nature is the female menstrual cycle. The cycle, which occurs approximately every 28 days, was originally associated with the cycles of the moon. Women in Eastern cultures would take themselves away from their normal routines while they were menstruating to relax and indulge in activities such as embroidery or other restful activities. In the West, women continue to 'work through' menstruation, but if they could relax for the first two days of the menstrual cycle they would experience fewer symptoms of PMT, irritability and emotional outbursts.

We are constantly trying to over-ride nature, but more and more of us are beginning to realise that we are just not powerful enough to fight against these elements. If we work with them, our life becomes much easier. Those who achieve this will tell you they wish they had done so sooner. This admission is the same from those now working with the principles of Chi Pilates.

The organs associated with water are the kidneys and the bladder. Both organs are responsible for looking after the waterworks in the body. They give us our strength and willpower for survival and determine the strength of our constitution. The kidneys govern our ability to reproduce, give birth and assist growth. Overindulgence in any way, be it overworking, drinking too much (alcohol) or lack of relaxation or sleep will result in the dysfunction of the kidneys. Typical symptoms are chronic thirst, premature greying of the hair (if not genetic) and impotence.

The kidney channel runs from a point in the middle of the ball of the foot. This point is known as K1 (kidney 1). It runs up the inside of the ankle, inside the leg, through the groin and up the front of the body to the collarbone. The old wives' tale that walking in bare feet would affect your kidneys, was correct.

Running close to the kidney channel are the inner thigh muscles, core stability muscles, the reproductive organs, the stomach and the chest (pectoralis). They are all vulnerable if there is energy deficiency within the kidney channel.

Right: in the West, women continue to 'work through' menstruation, but if they could relax for the first two days of the menstrual cycle they would experience fewer symptoms of PMT, irritability and emotional outbursts.

LOOKING AT THE DEEPER PICTURE – EAST AND WEST RE-UNITED

The bladder along with the kidneys regulate the excretion of waste from the body.

The bladder energy channel runs close to the roots of the peripheral nerves and autonomic nervous system. The function of the bladder, therefore, has a direct influence on this system and on the hormonal system, which is regulated by the pituitary gland. When we experience fear or anxiety our bladder is affected. How many times do you go to the toilet prior to an important appointment or when your nervous? Our emotions play an important role in the function of the bladder.

The bladder channel starts at the corner of the eye. It travels over the head and down the neck. It then separates into two channels running alongside the spine into the buttocks and down the back of the legs into the ankle bone, the outside of the foot and finishes at the little toe.

The muscles located in that area – the calf muscle (gastrocnemius) hamstrings, gluteus maximus, paraspinals, latissimus dorsi and trapezius – will all be affected if there is disharmony in the bladder energy. Tight muscles restrict energy flow, so if any of these muscles are tight it will have an affect on the function of the bladder.

Other signs of deficiency in kidneys/bladder:

- *Low back pain.*
- *Red tongue.*
- *Brittle bones.*
- *Night sweats.*
- *Dark urine.*
- *Cold limbs.*
- *Dark rings under the eyes.*

Exercises for the kidney/bladder:

Balance	Forward roll
Ankle circles	Warm-up
Knee lifts	Spinal flexion
Shoulder bridge	Roll-up
Leg circles	Inner thighs
Single leg	Oblique
Double leg	Hamstrings
Roll-down	Breast stroke
Swan dive	

Below: balance exercise.

PILATES EXERCISES

Below: read through the five principles regularly. Always come back to the starting postural position when you have finished an exercise.

Below: you will require a mat or thick towel to lie on; enough room to place your arms over your head and out to your side; two hand towels; a soft ball or pillow and a scarf or resistance band.

EXERCISE REQUISITES

You will require a mat or thick towel to lie on; enough room to place your arms over your head and out to your side; two hand towels; and a soft ball or pillow. Wear something comfortable so you are free to move. No trainers required.

Read through the five principles regularly. Always come back to the starting postural position when you have finished an exercise.

The important thing is the quality of your move rather than the amount of repetitions you do.

The results are achieved by repeating the exercises with good form. If you progress too quickly, you will lose your form and the essence of the exercise.

Initially you will have a lot to think about and it may seem confusing. Work with one principle at a time until you can work effortlessly with it then add another until you can perform the exercise using all five principles.

Aim to perform 10 repetitions effortlessly.

DO NOT use momentum or any forced movements. If you force a move, you will be tearing the fibres you are trying to lengthen and thereby wasting your efforts. Move with control and without tension.

Imagine someone is watching you – every move should look effortless. When you watch a dancer or gymnast, their moves flow gracefully; that is how Pilates should also be performed.

**Quality not quantity
Less is more**

PILATES EXERCISES

BALANCE

Essence of the exercise
To strengthen the whole musculoskeletal system.

Added benefits
- Builds awareness and improves balance.
- Gives space for the internal organs.
- Improves breathing technique.

Starting position
Standing.

- Posture check.
- Feet parallel.
- Feet in line with the knees.
- Knees in line with the hip bones.
- Pelvis in neutral.

Below: as the heels touch the floor keep the weight equally distributed between each leg and bend the knees. Breathing in to raise the body, up onto the balls of the feet, raising both arms up.

Right: look directly forward. This will also help stability.

PILATES EXERCISES

- Ribcage and shoulder blades down.
- Head sitting centrally on top of the shoulders.
- Breathing in to raise the body, up onto the balls of the feet, raising both arms up.
- Breathing out, pull up and in and lower the heels to the floor, circling the arms back by your side.
- As the heels touch the floor, keep the weight equally distributed between each leg and bend the knees.
- Repeat 5–10 times.

Guidelines
- Spine remains in neutral and you don't lean forward or backwards.
- Take your arms out to the side if it helps to maintain stability.
- Look directly forward. This will also help stability.
- When bending the knees, keep the knees apart and the arches of the foot lifted.

To challenge your balance, keep the heels off the floor until you have finished.

PILATES EXERCISES

FORWARD ROLL

Starting position
Sitting.

Essence of the exercise
To correctly articulate the spine from its neutral position, through flexion and back to neutral.

To strengthen and lengthen spinal musculature (paraspinals) while maintaining a neutral pelvis.

Added benefits
- Relaxes the nervous system.
- Massages the liver, spleen and kidneys.
- Increases blood supply to the brain.

- Breathe in to lengthen the neck.
- Breathe out, pull up and in, drop the head forward and begin to peel the spine forward one vertebra at a time. (Imagine your spine were a strip of velcro and you were stuck against a wall – peel the spine away slowly).
- Curl down and stop as soon as you feel any tension in the spine.
- Breathe in to stay.
- Breathe out, returning, coming up one vertebra at a time (sticking the velcro back onto the wall).

Guidelines
- Be careful not to allow the abdominals to relax when you are curled forward.
- Hip flexors (the crease at the top of the leg) remain relaxed
- Keep the pelvis in neutral while curling down and curling up.

Below: curl down and stop as soon as you feel any tension in the spine.

PILATES EXERCISES

SEATED TWIST AND TILT

Starting position
Sitting (option to sit on a chair or ball).

Essence of the exercise
To mobilise the spine using rotation from a seated position.
To strengthen the paraspinals and oblique muscles.

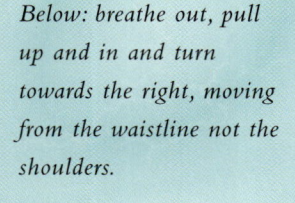

Below: breathe out, pull up and in and turn towards the right, moving from the waistline not the shoulders.

Added benefits
- Massages internal organs.
- Relieves back tension.

- Sit upright with a neutral spine, abdominals pulled in, ribcage and shoulder blades down. Clasp your hands gently in front of the chest at shoulder level.
- Breathe in to prepare.
- Breathe out, pull up and in and turn towards the right, moving from the waistline not the shoulders. Remember the action dolls, Barbie, Action Man etc. They could only turn from the waist. You do the same.
- Keep the abdominals pulled in and the shoulders relaxed. Your head should stay centrally positioned on top of your shoulders. As the body turns, the head turns also, but don't strain the neck.
- Breathe in to return.
- Breathe out, pull up and in, and tilt the pelvis into a 'c' curve of the spine.
- Breathe in to return the spine to neutral.
- Breathe out, pull up and in and rotate to the left.
- Repeat this five times to each side.

Guidelines
- Only turn as far as you can without force or straining.

PILATES EXERCISES

LYING ON YOUR BACK (SUPINE) AND CHECKING POSTURE

- Start by lying on your back with your knees bent.
- Feet parallel to one another.
- Feet in line with your knees (knees apart).
- Knees in line with your hip bones.
- Pelvis in 'neutral'.
- Arms are by your side and relaxed.
- Shoulder blades wide and down your back.
- Head resting centrally on top of the shoulders.

Checking your stability
- Breathe into the ribcage, lengthening the neck.
- Breathe out, pulling up and in, sliding the ribcage down.
- Shoulder blades wide and down.

Below: start by lying on your back with your knees bent.

PILATES EXERCISES

WARM-UP – ON THE FLOOR

Essence of the exercise
To increase mobility within shoulder girdle while maintaining neutral. To strengthen stability while lengthening the legs

Starting position
Supine.

Added benefits
- Calms the mind.
- Improves lung capacity.

LEVEL 1

- Breathe in. Raise the arms up towards the ceiling, keeping the shoulders and ribcage down.
- Breathe out, pull up and in and take the arms behind you in a 'v' shape, sliding the ribcage down and stabilising the shoulder blades.
- Breathe in again to raise the arms back up to the ceiling.
- Breathe out, pull up and in and bring the arms back by your side.
- Repeat this five times.

Guidelines
- Pelvis stays in neutral.
- Keep the shoulder blades wide and relaxed.
- Don't allow the ribcage to pop up as the arms go behind the head.
- When the arms are over the head they should feel as though they are suspended and being held by the shoulder girdle. It should feel as though you could stay there forever. Everyone's range of movement will be different. Only take the arms as far back as you can maintain stability.

Below: breathe in. Raise the arms up towards the ceiling, keeping the shoulders and ribcage down. Breathe out, pull up and in and take the arms behind you in a 'v' shape, sliding the ribcage down and stabilising the shoulder blades.

PILATES EXERCISES

Level 2

- Breathe in and lengthen the neck.
- Breathe out. Pull up and in. Slide right leg along the floor only as far as you can maintain neutral pelvis.
- Breathe in to stay.
- Breathe out. Pull up and in. Slide the right leg back in. Pelvis remains still.
- Repeat with the left leg.
- Repeat this five times on each leg.

Guidelines

- Pelvis remains in neutral
- 3 o'clock and 9 o'clock on your clockface should not be rocking when changing legs.
- Try to keep the neck long and relaxed and still.
- The aim is to move the legs independently without moving the spine. The less movement you make within the torso, the more stable you are.

Level 3

- Breathe in. Raise the arms.
- Breathe out. Pull up and in. Take arms behind and slide right leg away.
- Breathe in. Raise the arms.
- Breathe out. Pull up and in. Lower the arms and return the leg.
- Repeat, sliding the left leg away.
- Repeat 5–10 times.

Guidelines

- When the arms are behind the head one leg is extended.
- When the arms are by your side, both legs are in.
- Pelvis remains in neutral and stable throughout.
- Ribcage is down
- Abdominals are contracted throughout, especially during the movements.

Progression

Take both legs out together.

Above: the warm up; level 2 (top), level 3 (middle) and the progression (bottom).

PILATES EXERCISES

Above: start to circle the foot around very, very slowly. Taking it as far as you can, go to the maximum. The lower and upper parts of your leg should stay completely still so that the movement comes directly from the ankle joint. Do five circles each way

ANKLE CIRCLES

The muscles on the outer side of the ankle weaken as we get older, which is why so many older people are prone to going over on their feet and spraining their ankles. This exercise is great for strengthening them.
It also demonstrates clearly that it is far more difficult to execute an exercise slowly rather than quickly.

Follow the instructions but, when you have finished, just try to do the exercise quickly and notice the difference.

Essence of the exercise
To free the ankle joint, increasing its mobility.
To strengthen the muscles, ligaments and tendons surrounding the ankle joint.
To work the muscles of the lower leg.

Starting position
Supine.

- Breathe in and lengthen the neck. Hinge the right leg in towards the chest and hold around the knee – this will help to stabilise the upper leg while the ankle is moving.
- Breathe out. Pull up and in. Rotate the foot as described below.
- Breathe in while still.
- Breathe out during the move.
- Start to circle the foot around very, very slowly. Taking it is as far as you can, go to the maximum. The lower and upper parts of your leg should stay completely still so that the movement comes directly from the ankle joint. Do five circles each way.

Guidelines
- Keep the jaw and facial muscles relaxed.
- Keep the other leg in alignment with your hip.

PILATES EXERCISES

SPINAL FLEXION

Essence of the exercise
To correctly articulate the cervical and thoracic spine.
To strengthen the abdominals while keeping the pelvis in neutral.

Starting position
Supine.

- Breathe in. Lengthen the neck.
- Breathe out. Pull up and in. Slide the ribcage towards the hips flexing forward and look towards your knees. Your hands slide down past the body, off the floor and towards your feet. Keep the shoulder blades wide in the back, abdominals pulled in and pelvis in neutral.
- Breathe in to return.
- Breathe out to release.
- Repeat 5–10 times.

Guidelines
- Maintain the relationship of the head and shoulders.
- Maintain a natural curve in the spine and neck when lifting off the floor.
- Only come up as high as you can maintaining stability and the neutral pelvis.
- Take care not to grip in the hip flexors.
- Abdomen stays flat and pulled in.

Modification
Place the hands behind the head to support the head and to release any tension in the neck.

Above: slide the ribcage towards the hips flexing forward and look towards your knees. Your hands slide down past the body, off the floor and towards your feet. Keep the shoulder blades wide in the back, abdominals pulled in and pelvis in neutral.

PILATES EXERCISES

KNEE LIFTS

Essence of the exercise
To strengthen the abdominals, keeping the pelvis in neutral.
To lengthen the lumbar region of the spine, while maintaining neutral pelvis.

Starting position
Supine.

LEVEL 1

- Breathe in. Lengthen the neck. Hinge the right leg up into the tabletop position.
- Breathe out. Pull up and in. Bring right leg back down.
- Breathe in. Lift the left leg up into tabletop position.
- Breathe out, pull up and in, place the foot back down.
- Repeat 5–10 times with each leg.

Modifications
Should you have difficulty in keeping the pelvis in neutral when lowering the leg, work from the imprinted spine.

LEVEL 2

- Breathe in, lengthen the neck and lift the right leg up into tabletop position.
- Breathe out, pull up and in and hinge left leg up to join the right.
- Breathe in to stay.
- Breathe out, pull up and in and bring the right leg down, followed by the left leg.
- Repeat 5–10 times.

Alternate the leading leg each time.

Guidelines
- Maintain stability in the torso while lifting the second leg and also while returning feet to floor.
- Watch the pelvis doesn't tilt.
- Upper body remains relaxed and stable.
- Shoulders and neck remain long and relaxed.

Below: breathe in. Lengthen the neck. Hinge the right leg up into the tabletop position.

Breathe out. Pull up and in and bring the left leg up to join the right.

PILATES EXERCISES

Above: the hundred; level 3, advanced level.

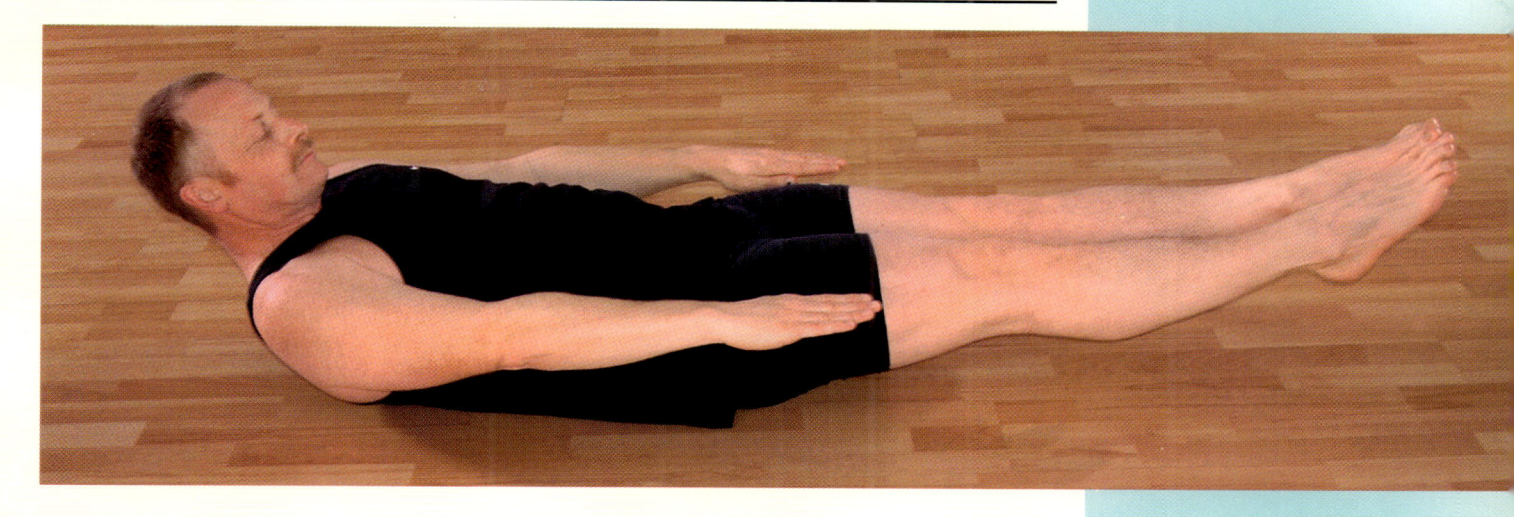

THE HUNDRED

Essence of the exercise
To stabilise the pelvis against the weight of the legs.
Helps to co-ordinate breathing with movement.
Staccato breathing helps to replenish the blood cells with oxygen while in a fixed position.
To strengthen the abdominals while keeping the spine in flexion.

Starting position
Supine.

LEVEL 1

- Breathe in and lengthen the neck.
- Breathe out and pull up and in. Slide ribcage towards hips and raise the upper body to look towards the knees. Raise arms off the floor, parallel to the body.
- Breathe in for five short breaths through the nose (as though you are sniffing when you have a cold).
- Breathe out for five out-breaths through the mouth.(as though you were blowing out five candles).
- During this count, beat the arms from the shoulder, keeping the hands strong at the end of the wrists and the elbows soft.
- Repeat this 10 times (total count of 100).

Guidelines
As soon as you feel tension in the neck, place the head down but continue to co-ordinate the breath with the beat of the arms for the full 100.

PILATES EXERCISES

Above: breathe out, pull up and in, slide ribcage towards hips to flex upper body and look towards the knees.

Level 2

- Breathe in. Lengthen the neck. Raise one leg into the tabletop position.
- Breathe out, pull up and in and bring the other leg up (work initially from the imprinted spine until your strength improves to maintain neutral).
- Breathe in to stay.
- Breathe out, pull up and in, slide ribcage towards hips to flex upper body and look towards the knees.
- Arms adjacent to the body, palms down.
- Breathe in for five counts, out for five counts. In through the nose; out through the mouth.
- Repeat 10 times (total count 100)

Guidelines

- Rest the head if there is tension in the neck.
- Modify the legs by bringing them back down to the floor should they begin to tire during the 100.
- Continue counting for the full 100.
- Keep the abdominals pulled in.

Level 3 – advanced level

As Level 2 with extended legs.

As you improve your strength, the legs can be lowered to a point where the abdominals are challenged.

PILATES EXERCISES

SHOULDER BRIDGE

Essence of the exercise
Strengthens lower back, abdominals and hamstrings. Improves flexibility of the whole spinal column. Correctly articulates the spine from the tailbone while under the weight of gravity.

Added benefits
- Nourishes the nerves throughout the spine.
- Massages the heart and lungs.
- Stimulates the thyroid gland which regulates your metabolic rate.

Starting position
Supine.

Below: breathe out, pull up and in tilting the pelvis into the imprinted spine, then raise the bottom off the floor, lifting the hips towards the ceiling.

PILATES EXERCISES

LEVEL 1 – (SHOULDER BRIDGE PREPARATION EXERCISE)

Place ball or pillow between the knees. Hands are down by your side, palms down to help keep the shoulder blades braced to the floor.

- Breathe in. Lengthen the neck.
- Breathe out, pull up and in and tilt the pelvis into the imprinted spine.
- Breathe in to stay.
- Breathe out, pull up and in and bring the pelvis back to neutral.
- Repeat this two or three times first in order to warm the lower spine and to allow time to focus your mind on where you're working. This exercise alone can help correct an over-arched back.
- Repeat 5–10 times.

Guidelines
- Don't be tempted to squeeze the buttocks during this.
- Keep hold of the ball/pillow. This keeps the legs in alignment.

LEVEL 2 – (FULL SHOULDER BRIDGE EXERCISE)

- Breathe in and lengthen the neck.
- Breathe out and pull up and in. Tilt the pelvis into the imprinted spine then raise the bottom off the floor, lifting the hips towards the ceiling and coming up through the spine vertebra by vertebra.
- Breathe in to stop.
- Breathe out and pull up and in. Come back towards the floor again vertebra by vertebra, coming down through the imprint and finishing off back in the neutral position.
- Repeat 5–10 times.

Guidelines
- Feet closer to the bottom will help engage the abdominals and back muscles.
- Feet placed further away will activate the hamstrings and buttocks.
- Always breathe out while moving the spine.
- Knees travel forward towards the toes as you lift off the floor.
- Keep the shoulder blades wide and down.
- Heels of the feet stay down.
- Don't over-extend. Only go up as far as is comfortable.
- Neck remains long – avoid pressure on cervical spine.

Once you can perform this exercise effortlessly, for five repetitions, begin Level 3 to increase your stamina.

LEVEL 3

When in full bridge position, stay there for 1–5 breaths.
Repeat 3–5 times.

PILATES EXERCISES

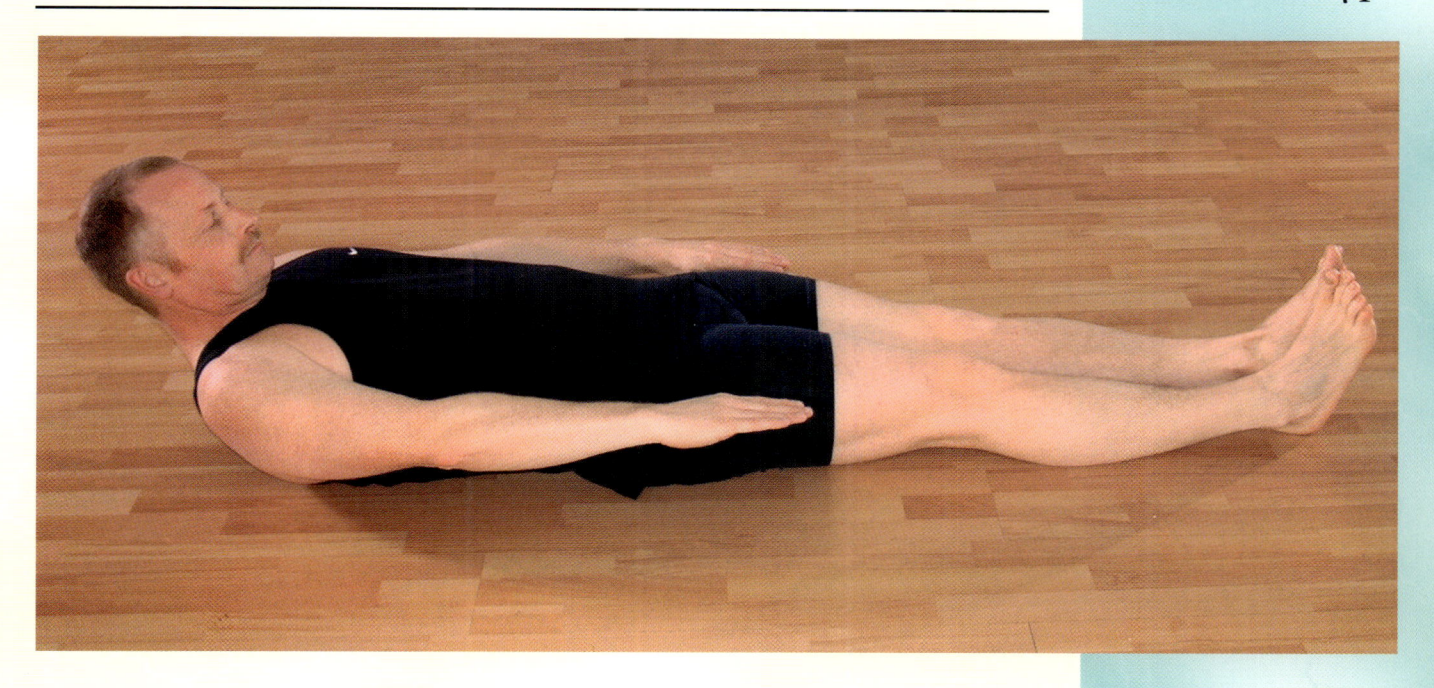

ROLL UP

Essence of the exercise
Correctly articulates the spine using the abdominals efficiently. Encourages the efficient movement of the pelvis on the thigh bone (femur).

Starting position
Supine.

LEVEL 1

- Breathe in and lengthen the neck.
- Breathe out, pull up and in and slide both legs away slowly to maintain pelvic stability (should you begin to lose the neutral pelvis, keep the knees slightly bent). Keep the legs and feet parallel.
- Breathe in and raise the arms towards the ceiling (keep the shoulders down).
- Breathe out, pull up and in and take the arms behind the head (keep ribcage down).
- Breathe in, lengthen the neck and begin to raise the arms again towards the ceiling.
- Breathe out, pull up and in and slide the ribcage towards the hips, lifting the head and shoulders to look towards the toes. The arms come right down by your side, keeping the pelvis in neutral and not gripping in the hip flexors at the top of the leg.
- Breathe in to raise the arms back towards the ceiling (keep looking towards the toes).
- Breathe out, pull up and in and take the body and the arms back.
- Repeat this 5–10 times.

Above: breathe out, pull up and in and slide the ribcage towards the hips, lifting the head and shoulders to look towards the toes. The arms come right down by your side, keeping the pelvis in neutral and not gripping in the hip flexors at the top of the leg.

PILATES EXERCISES

Below: reach towards the toes, keeping the shoulder blades down, arms parallel to the legs and in line with the shoulders, creating a letter 'u' on its side.

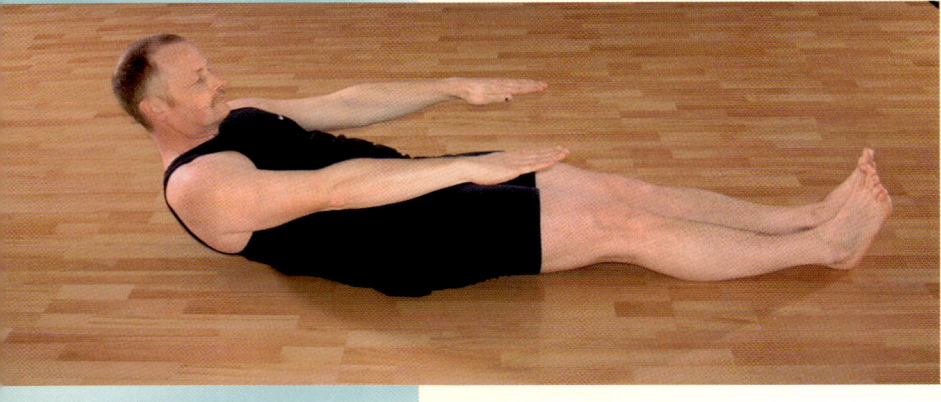

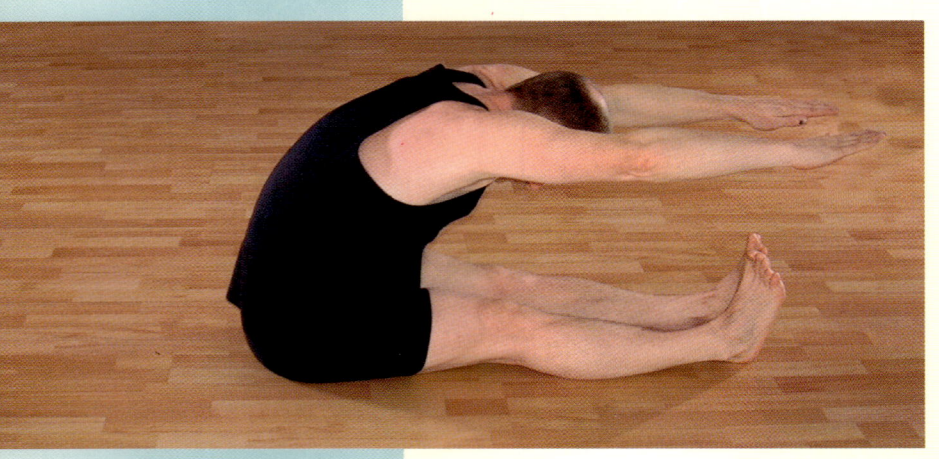

LEVEL 2

As Level 1 only, as your strength and flexibility improve, you can:

- Roll up on the out-breath as far as the body allows without jerking, or using any momentum. As you roll up, tilt the pelvis to imprint the spine as you articulate the spine off the floor.
- Reach towards the toes, keeping the shoulder blades down, arms parallel to the legs and in line with the shoulders, creating a letter 'u' on its side.
- Breathe in to start moving back
- Breathe out, pull up and in as you return through the imprint back down onto the floor.
- Repeat 5–10 times.

Guidelines:
- NEVER use momentum.
- Abdominals remain pulled in throughout.
- Keep a natural curve in the cervical area of the spine as the head lifts.
- Keep the shoulder blades down as your reach forward.
- If you can, keep the legs straight and the toes turned up towards the ceiling throughout. This will add the benefit of a hamstring stretch.

PILATES EXERCISES

LEG CIRCLES

Essence of the exercise
To correctly articulate the femur within the hip joint while maintaining a neutral and stable pelvis. This enhances hip movement and produces fluid around the joint for freer mobility.

- Breathe in to lengthen the neck.
- Breathe out and lift the right leg up into the tabletop position.
- Breathe in and take the leg towards the other leg.
- Breathe out, pull up and in and circle the leg around.
- Repeat this three times in each direction then repeat on the other leg.

Guidelines
- Place your hands on the hip joints to check your stability.
- Keep the opposite hip still.
- Keep to small circles to begin with.

INNER THIGHS

Essence of the exercise
To lengthen and strengthen the inner thigh muscles correctly while keeping the pelvis in neutral.

Starting position
Prone

- Breathe in to lengthen the neck
- Breathe out, pull up and in and drop both knees out to the side, maintaining a neutral pelvis.
- Breathe in to stay.
- Breathe out, pull up and in and bring the legs back to their original position.
- Repeat 5–10 times.

Guidelines
- Keep the neutral spine throughout
- Shoulders and neck remain relaxed.

Above: breathe out, pull up and in and drop both knees out to the side, maintaining a neutral pelvis.

Below: breathe in and take the leg towards the other leg. Breathe out, pull up and in and circle the leg around.

PILATES EXERCISES

LEG LIFTS (SINGLE LEG PREPARATION EXERCISE)

Essence of the exercise
To strengthen core stability while extending the weight of the legs away from the hips.

Starting position
Supine (ball or pillow between the knees).

Below: breathe in and bring the extended leg back, placing the foot back on the floor.

Prep 1

- Breathe in and release the neck.
- Breathe out, pull up and in and extend one leg off the floor.
- Breathe in and bring the extended leg back, placing the foot back on the floor.
- Breathe out, pull up and in and extend the other leg away.
- Repeat 10 times.

Guidelines
- Keep stability and neutral pelvis.
- Keep both knees in line.
- Keep the neck long and relaxed.

Prep 2

As Prep 1. Place the hands behind your head.

- Breathe in to lengthen the neck.
- Breathe out, pull up and in, slide the ribcage towards the hips and raise the head to look towards the knees.
- Breathe in to stay.
- Breathe out and extend one leg away.
- Breathe in and bring the leg back.
- Breathe out, pull up and in and extend the other leg away.
- Repeat 5–10 times.

Guidelines
- Neck, shoulders and arms relaxed.
- Abdominals pulled in throughout.
- Any tension in the neck – rest the head down.

PILATES EXERCISES

SINGLE-LEG STRETCH

Starting position
Supine.

- Breathe in, lengthen the neck and raise one leg into the tabletop position.
- Breathe out, pull up and in and bring the other leg up. Pelvis is now in the imprinted spine position.
- Breathe in to lengthen the neck.
- Breathe out to raise the head and shoulders, sliding the ribcage down and placing the hands on the left leg, the left hand positioned towards the left ankle, the right hand positioned on the inside of the left knee. (This maintains alignment and stability in the legs while working.)
- Once in your starting position, breathe in to prepare.
- Breathe out and pull up and in to extend the right leg away, maintaining the imprint.
- Breathe in on the return and swap hands to the left leg.
- Breathe out, pull up and in to extend the left leg away.
- Repeat 10 times.

On completion
- Breathe in to hold the tabletop position.
- Breathe out to release the head and shoulders down and to bring the legs down with control one at a time.

Guidelines
- Abdominals pulled in and not popping up
- Keep neck relaxed and long.
- Maintain the imprint while extending the legs.
- Any tension in the neck – place the head back down.

Above: breathe out to raise the head and shoulders, sliding the ribcage down and placing the hands on the left leg, the left hand positioned towards the left ankle and the right hand positioned on the inside of the left knee.

PILATES EXERCISES

OBLIQUE

Essence of the exercise
The emphasis is on the rotation of the spine. This is a good exercise for those with scoliosis.

Below: Level 1- breathe out, pull up and in and take the right rib across towards the left hip bone.

Starting position
Supine with the hands behind the head, knees bent, legs apart, pelvis neutral.

LEVEL 1

- Breathe in to lengthen neck.
- Breathe out, pull up and in and slide the ribs towards the hips. Raise the head and shoulders to look forward between the legs.
- Breathe in to stay.
- Breathe out, pull up and in and take the right rib across towards the left hip bone.
- Breathe in to return to centre.
- Breathe out, pull up and in and take left rib across towards the right hip bone.
- Repeat to each side five times.

LEVEL 2

Starting position
Supine.

- As Level 1, only feet are on the floor, knees in line with the hips.
- Repeat five times to each side.

LEVEL 3

Starting position
Supine with legs in a tabletop position.

- Repeat five times to each side.

LEVEL 4 – ADVANCED LEVEL

- Adding in the single leg stretch pattern.
- Repeat five times to each side.

Guidelines
- The pelvis remains in neutral. Both hips stay stable.
- Arms stay relaxed to support head and to keep the chest open.
- Lifting and rotating from the mid-torso.
- Keep the relationship between the head and shoulders.

PILATES EXERCISES

77

Left: Level 2 - as Level 1, only feet are on the floor, knees in line with the hips.

Level 3 - supine with legs in a tabletop position.

Level 4 - adding in the single leg stretch pattern.

Below: Level 1 - lengthen the neck and raise the arms overhead in a 'v' shape.

Level 3 - start from a tabletop position – upper body flexed forward.

Right: Level 4 - extend both legs away while raising the arms overhead.

PILATES EXERCISES

DOUBLE-LEG STRETCH

Essence of the exercise
Challenges the strength of the abdominals to maintain pelvic alignment while the body is in flexion and the legs are off the floor. Further challenges the neuromuscular ability when adding in the movements of the arms and legs.

Starting position
Supine.

LEVEL 1

- Breathe in, lengthen the neck and raise the arms overhead in a 'v' shape (palms of the hands facing one another).
- Breathe out, pull up and in, rotating the arms from the shoulder (palms facing away from one another). Circle the arms back round by your side (palms will finish facing the body again).
- Repeat 10 times.

LEVEL 2

- Start with the legs in a tabletop position and keep them there throughout the exercise, maintaining a neutral pelvis.
- The modification is to work in the imprinted spine position.

LEVEL 3

- Start from a tabletop position – upper body flexed forward.

LEVEL 4 – ADVANCED

- Extend both legs away while raising the arms overhead.
- Bring both legs back to a tabletop position as you circle the arms around.

Guidelines
- Maintain stability within the torso and head.
- Keep inner thighs and feet together once the legs are off the floor.
- Keep the neck lengthened and relaxed.

PILATES EXERCISES

Above: breathe in to swing the leg gently back to the front.

SIDE-LYING HIP EXTENSION

Starting position
Side-lying with the knees up at 90' to the hip. Keep the spine in neutral. The position you are in should be identical to your position when lying on your back with both legs up in tabletop – abdominals pulled in, waistline light against the floor, shoulders level with one another, your head supported by a towel or your arm to keep it centrally positioned above the shoulders. Place a soft ball or rolled-up towel behind the top knee.

Essence of the exercise
To free up tightness in the hip extensors. To strengthen the stabilising muscles of the torso while in a side-lying position.

- Breathe in to raise the leg to hip height.
- Breathe out, pull up and in and take the leg back, maintaining a neutral spine.
- Breathe in to swing the leg gently back to the front and repeat this 10 times.

Guidelines
- Watch that you don't over-arch the lumbar spine when taking the leg back.
- Keep the abdominals pulled in throughout
- There should be no tension in the upper body.
- Keep your foot stable at the end of the leg. Try not to dangle it.

PILATES EXERCISES

Above: Leg exercises 1 - point the toes of the top leg.

Leg exercises 2 - lengthen and lift both legs off the floor together.

Leg exercises 3 - breathe out, pull up and in and circle the leg.

LEG EXERCISES

Starting position
Side-lying.

Essence of the exercise
Proper adduction and abduction of the hip.

EXERCISE 1

- Point the toes of the top leg.
- Breathe in to lift and lengthen the leg. Flex the foot.
- Breathe out and pull up and in to lower the leg down. Point the toes.
- Breathe in to lift, breathe out to lower.
- Point the toes on the way up.
- Flex the foot on the way down.
- Repeat 8–10 times.

EXERCISE 2

- Breathe in to prepare.
- Breathe out and pull up and in to lengthen and lift both legs off the floor together.
- Breathe in to bring them back down.
- Keep upper body relaxed
- Repeat 8–10 times.

EXERCISE 3

- Breathe in to raise the leg hip height, pointing the toes away.
- Breathe out, pull up and in and circle the leg.
- Breathe in to stay.
- Breathe out to circle.
- Repeat three times one way, three times the other.
- Stay still on the in-breath.
- Only move on the out-breath.
- Keep lengthening the leg away from the hip.

Guidelines
- Pelvis remains stable and in neutral.
- Keep the upper body relaxed during the whole of the leg exercises.

DON'T FORGET TO DO THE LEG EXERCISES ON BOTH LEGS.

PILATES EXERCISES

HAMSTRING STRETCH
(with band or scarf)

Essence of the exercise
To re-lengthen and strengthen the hamstrings.

Starting position
Supine. One leg in tabletop position with band or scarf cradling the foot.

- Breathe in and lengthen the neck.
- Breathe out and pull up and in. Lengthen the leg so it's parallel to the floor.
- Breathe in to stay.
- Breathe out to raise the leg towards the ceiling to a point of tension.
- Breathe in to stay.
- Breathe out to lengthen the leg back towards the floor.
- Repeat five times on each leg.

Guidelines
- Neck, shoulders and arms remain relaxed.
- Pelvis remains in neutral.
- Keep the foot flexed within the band throughout, lengthening the leg through the heel.
- The knee on the leg you are stretching should be angled towards the shoulder and not towards the mid-line of the body.
- Avoid tension behind the knee
- Keep both hips down.

Below: breathe out to raise the leg towards the ceiling to a point of tension.

Below: breathe out, pull up and in and tilt the pelvis (pull on your tail). Loose the curves of the spine, creating a 'c' curve. Breathe in to return to a postural position.

Right: breathe out, pull up and in and continue tilting the pelvis lowering the spine to the floor, vertebra by vertebra, until the whole back is down.

PILATES EXERCISES

ROLL-DOWN

Essence of the exercise
To strengthen and lengthen the abdominals while under the force of gravity. To mobilise and strengthen the low back.

Starting position
Sitting with the pelvis in neutral.

Visualisation
Tail between the legs. When tilting the pelvis, imagine you are pulling on your tail to bring your tail bone from underneath you.

LEVEL 1
- Breathe in to prepare.
- Breathe out, pull up and in and tilt the pelvis (pull on your tail). Loose the curves of the spine, creating a 'c' curve. Breathe in to return to a postural position.
- Repeat 5–10 times.

LEVEL 2
- Breathe in to prepare.
- Breathe out, pull up and in, pull on your tail, tilting the pelvis to create the 'c' curve of the spine.
- Breathe in to stay in the 'c' curve.
- Breathe out, pull up and in and continue tilting the pelvis lowering the spine to the floor, vertebra by vertebra, until the whole back is down.
- Breathe in to return the spine to neutral.
- Breathe out to come back up to sitting.
- Repeat 8–10 times.

Three ways to bring yourself up off the floor, from lying on your back to sitting.

Roll over and up
- *From your back, roll over onto your side and ease yourself up to sitting.*
- *This way is advisable for anyone with low back pain. As the abdominals and back get stronger, move to the next method.*

Rock 'n' roll
- *While on your back, bring both knees into the chest and hold behind the knees.*
- *Breathe in to prepare and, on the out-breath, pull up and in and rock 'n' roll yourself up to sitting.*

Roll up
- *From your back.*
- *Breathe in to prepare.*
- *Breathe out, pull up and in and slide the ribcage towards the hips to flex the upper body, imprinting the spine as you curl up from the floor to sitting.*

PILATES EXERCISES

HIP ROLL

Starting position
Supine.

Essence of the exercise
To establish efficient rotation of the spine while maintaining good pelvic alignment.

- Breathe in to prepare and lengthen the neck.
- Breathe out, pull up and in.
- Take both legs to the right side, keeping the knees and feet together.
- The head turns to look down the left arm.
- Take the legs only as far as you can to maintain your stability and relaxation in the upper body.
- Breathe in to stay.
- Breathe out, pull up and in and bring the ribcage back towards the floor – the hips will follow then the legs and head come back to centre.
- Repeat to the left.
- Repeat five times each side.

Guidelines
- Shoulders remain on the floor at all times.
- The upper body stays relaxed.
- Feet and knees stay together.
- Make sure you have checked that your abdominals are pulled in before you move.

Above: take both legs to the right side, keeping the knees and feet together. The head turns to look down the left arm. Take the legs only as far as you can to maintain stability and relaxation in the upper body.

PILATES EXERCISES

Observation 1
When taking the legs to the side, it is their weight that initiates the lift in the hips. The movement of the hips then initiates the ribs to rotate.

On the return, the movement is initiated from the ribcage using the strength of the oblique muscle which draws the hips back and then the weight of the legs.

Observation 2
Your range of movement may be good, but your strength may not be, so watch that you don't take the knees too far that you can't bring them back again without recruiting the muscles in the upper body.

Observation 3
When moving from centre think:
LEGS – HIPS – RIBCAGE.

On return think:
RIBCAGE – HIPS – LEGS.

LEVEL 2

As Level 1.

Starting position Supine. Legs in tabletop position.

PILATES EXERCISES

LIZARD

Starting position
Lying on your front with knees apart and bent, feet together. Place a ball or pillow between the feet. Hands are near to the shoulders, but away from the body, elbows down on the floor. Should this cause any discomfort in the lower part of the back, do this with the forehead resting on a pillow, keeping the head centrally positioned on top of the shoulders. Shoulder blades are down towards the hips and the abdominals are pulled up.

Essence of the exercise
To mobilise the spine during rotation. To strengthen the abdominals and spine during co-ordinated movement.

- Breathe in to prepare.
- Breathe out, pull up and in and take the feet towards the floor on the right side, keeping the shoulder blades down. Lift the hip and elbow away from the floor as you rotate further, taking the feet as far down towards the floor as you can without loosing control or straining.
- Breathe in to stay.
- Breathe out, pull up and in and bring the ribs back towards the floor, followed by the hips. Lastly the legs come back to the centre.
- Repeat to the other side.
- Repeat this five times to each side.

Guidelines
- Stay relaxed and in control.
- Head stays centrally on top of the shoulders – watch the chin doesn't drop towards the chest.
- Abdominals stay pulled up throughout.
- If you feel any kind of pinching in the lower back, check these first before resorting to doing the exercise with the head down.
- If you are experiencing any discomfort during this exercise in the lower back, check the following points:
  - Are your abdominals pulled in? The answer should be yes
  - Are you pushing your hips into the floor at any time? The answer should be no.
  - Are your shoulder blades staying down during the exercise? The answer should be yes
  - Are you holding any tension in the neck? The answer should be no.

If your answers do not correspond, try to resolve them and, if the discomfort remains, do the exercise with the head supported off the floor. Alternatively, place a folded towel under the hips to help lengthen the lower back.

Far left: your range of movement may be good, but your strength may not be, so watch that you don't take the knees too far that you can't bring them back again without recruiting the muscles in the upper body.

Below: lying on your front with knees apart and bent, feet together. Lift the hip and elbow away from the floor as you rotate further, taking the feet as far down towards the floor as you can without loosing control or straining.

PILATES EXERCISES

STAR

Essence of the exercise
To lengthen the paraspinals.
To challenge the neuromuscular patterns.

Starting position
Prone.

LEVEL 1

- Breathe in to prepare.
- Breathe out, pull up and in and lift one leg 2 inches off the floor. Lengthen away from the hip, keeping the leg straight and the pelvis neutral.
- Breathe in to relax the leg down.
- Breathe out to lift the other leg.
- Repeat this three times on each leg.

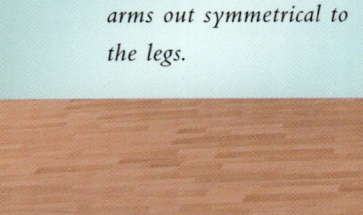

LEVEL 2

As Level 1, only take both arms out symmetrical to the legs.

- Breathe in to prepare.
- Breathe out, pull up and in, lift one leg and the opposite arm 2 inches off the floor.
- Breathe in to relax them down.
- Breathe out to raise the other arm and leg together.
- Repeat five times each side.
- Keep both hips on the floor, pelvis neutral.
- Keep lengthening away from the centre.

Below: breathe out pull up and in lift one leg 2 inches off the floor. Lengthen away from the hip keeping the leg straight and the pelvis neutral.

As Level 1 only take both arms out symmetrical to the legs.

PILATES EXERCISES

PRESS-UPS

There are various ways to help strengthen the arms and upper body, but none are quite as efficient as the push-up. This exercise also strengthens the abdominals and the lower back if executed correctly.

It is therefore important NOT to do a level which is beyond your capabilities. If each level is approached intelligently, then you will succeed in working at your own level safely and getting results.

Essence of the exercise
To lengthen and strengthen the chest muscles (pectoralis). Lengthen and strengthen the triceps (the back of the arms). Strengthen all stabilising muscle groups to maintain a neutral spine.

If you have wrist, knee, hip or low back issues, follow Level 1 – the standing position.

The modification level should not be used until you can perform five repetitions effortlessly.

LEVEL 1

- Stand facing a wall, arms outstretched, hands spread, elbows extended but not locked out.
- Feet apart, weight of the body in the arms.
- Breathe in to bend at the elbows, bringing the chest closer to the wall.  
- Breathe out to push away from the wall.
- Repeat 8–10 times.

Above: Level 2 – breathe in to bend at the elbows, bringing the chest closer to the wall.

Left: Level 1 – the standing position.

PILATES EXERCISES

Above: Level 3 – slide the shoulder blades down towards the hips without forcing them. The spine should still be in its neutral position.

Guidelines
- If you are able to get close to the wall with your chest, take your feet further away.
- Maintain a neutral spine.

Level 2

- Starting on your hands and knees, spread hands and fingers so that you establish a good base for the upper body.
- Slide the shoulder blades down towards the hips without forcing them. Draw the abdomen up towards the spine. Imagine there is an ice pick pointing up towards the navel from below.

- Without moving the hands or the upper body, take the knees 6–12 inches further back behind the hips.
- Shoulders remain above the hands.
- The spine should still be in its neutral position.
- Breathe in to bend both elbows outwards one inch, 2 inches, 3 inches, lowering the upper body towards the floor
- Breathe out, pull up and in and push back up.

Only go down as far as the arms can hold the weight of the body. You may find you can get down, but remember you have to get back up again – with control and keeping spinal alignment.
- Repeat this 3–5 times and rest. Shake the wrists out.
- Repeat 3–5 times altogether.

Guidelines
- Maintain neutral spine throughout the exercise.
- Don't allow the hips or the head to drop
- Keep the elbows soft when pushing back up. Don't hyperextend.
- Be careful not to lose the stability in the shoulder blades when pushing back up.
- Keep the knees soft when in a full press-up position

Level 3

As Level 1, only adopting the full press-up position.

PILATES EXERCISES

BREAST STROKE

Essence of the exercise
To correctly extend the mid-back.

Starting position
Prone.

LEVEL 1 PREP 1

- Breathe in to slide the shoulder blades down towards the hips, adding slight adduction of the shoulder blades towards the spine (without force and without any pinching).
- Breathe out to release.
- Don't rest completely here – keep the arms lifted off the floor, abdominals connected and head raised.
- Repeat 8–10 times.

LEVEL 2

- Breathe in to slide the shoulder blades towards the hips, raising the chest away from the floor.
- Breathe out to lower the chest down.
- Repeat 8–10 times.

LEVEL 3

- Breathe in to slide shoulder blades towards the hips, raising the chest away from the floor.
- Breathe out to stay, taking the right arm out to the side. Rotating at the shoulder, reach the arm forward, turning the thumbs to the ceiling and keeping the shoulder blades down.
- Breathe in to return the arm to your side.
- Breathe out to release.
- Repeat with the other arm.

LEVEL 4

As Level 1, but using both arms together.

Guidelines
- Keep abdominals pulled up throughout.
- Keep shoulder blades down.
- Keep the buttocks and legs relaxed.

Above: Level 1 - slide the shoulder blades down towards the hips.

Level 2 – slide the shoulder blades towards the hips, raising the chest away from the floor.

Below: Level 4 - using both arms together.

SWAN DIVE

Essence of the exercise
To fully extend the spine.

Starting position
Prone.

Preparation
- Hands start by the shoulders.
- Legs are slightly apart.
- Elbows down.
- Shoulder blades down.
- Head lifted, sitting centrally on top of the shoulders.
- Abdominals pulled up.

LEVEL 1 – PART 1

- Breathe in to slide the shoulder blades towards the hips, raising the chest away from the floor. Use the hands to support you as you come up a little higher, extending the elbows.
- Keep the shoulder blades down.
- Keep the elbows in.
- Keep abdominals pulled up.
- Breathe out to come back down onto the elbows and stay as you raise the arms off the floor.
- Place the arms back on the floor.
- Repeat 5–10 times.

LEVEL 1 – PART 2

- Breathe in to keep upper body relaxed.
- Breathe out, pull up and in and raise right leg off the floor from the hip.

PILATES EXERCISES

- Maintain neutral pelvis.
- Both hips stay down.
- Lengthen the back of the knee.
- Point the toe.
- Upper body stays totally stable and relaxed.
- Breathe in to return the leg to the floor.
- Breathe out to lift the other leg.

- Repeat five times each leg.

Once you have total stability in the pelvis and you are not recruiting muscles in the upper body when lifting the leg, try lifting both legs together.

LEVEL 2

- Breathe in to slide shoulder blades down and raise chest away from the floor.
- Breathe out to return to elbows while raising the legs off the floor.
- Extend the arms out in front, turning the thumbs up towards the ceiling. (When doing this, think of yourself as the leg of a rocking chair – as one end rises the other end falls. You are working from your centre and fully extending the spine.)
- Repeat 8–10 times.

Follow with back release
- When finishing this exercise, push up onto all fours.
- Knees apart, feet together.
- Sit back towards heels.
- Head down.
- Release the back and relax.
- Breathe into the back until you are comfortable to continue.

Above and below: to fully extend the spine follow the levels of the Swan dive exercise.

PILATES EXERCISES

TABLE BALANCE

Essence of the exercise
To strengthen stabilising muscles while maintaining neutral against gravity.

Starting position
On all fours.

LEVEL 1

- Breathe in.
- Breathe out and check your stability (pelvic floor, abdominals, ribcage, shoulder blades, head placement).
- Repeat this 5–10 times maintaining position.

Guidelines
- Head doesn't begin to drop
- Shoulders stay down.
- Watch you don't start sagging at the middle.
- Rest if your wrists become uncomfortable.

Modification for wrists
Should you experience discomfort in the wrists, try this other position (on your fist). If you have shoulder, elbow or wrist issues, come down onto your elbows but keep the spine in neutral.

LEVEL 2

- Breathe in to prepare and, as you exhale, check your stability and lengthen the right leg away along the floor, keeping your balance.

(Watch you don't compensate for your weight with the other leg or sink into the hip.)

- Repeat on the other side, always breathing out on the extension.

As your balance improves, this can be progressed so you extend the opposite arm to leg away at the same time, challenging your strength and stability.

LEVEL 3

As Level 2, only raising opposite leg and arm off the floor together when extended.
Be careful not to allow the spine to come out of neutral.

Below: breathe in to prepare and, as you exhale, check your stability and lengthen the right leg away along the floor, keeping your balance and then lift the left arm off the floor watching you don't compensate for your weight with the other leg or sink into the hip.

PILATES EXERCISES

ARM CIRCLES

Essence of the exercise
To lengthen the chest muscles (pectoralis) and strengthen the mid-back (mid-trapezius).
To challenge the strength of the abdominals while maintaining a neutral pelvis during rotation of the spine.

Starting position
Side-lying position with knees at 90°

- Breathe in to prepare.
- Breathe out, pull up and in and circle the top arm up over the head and make as full a circle as you can.
- Repeat 6–8 times in each direction.
- Roll over to the other side and repeat with the other arm.

Guidelines
- Keep the knees together. If you feel any movement in the knees then the pelvis has moved out of alignment and the lower back is vulnerable.
- Relax the arm. Don't tense it up while moving.
- Holding something light in the hand (a soft ball) can help to keep eye contact with the hand. It also helps to extend the arm, increasing the stretch.

Above: breathe out, pull up and in and circle the top arm up over the head and make as full a circle as you can.

INDEX

A
abdominal curl 8
abdominal distension 49
acupuncture 41
alignment 8–9, 11, 13, 14, 17, 22, 27, 35, 36, 42
America 7
anatomical terminology 10
anger 45
ankle circles 45, 47, 51, 55, 64
anterior movement 10
anxiety 23, 52, 55
appetite 49
Aristotle 14
arm circles 45, 47, 51, 93
autonomic nervous system 55
autumn 48, 50, 52

B
back 10–11, 35
balance 35, 45, 47, 49, 51, 53, 55, 58
belching 49
birth 52, 54
bladder 27, 42, 52–55
blood 9, 15, 23, 44–45, 46–47, 50, 51
bones 21, 55
bowel 27
breast stroke 47, 49, 51, 55
breathing 7, 9, 18, 23–26, 42, 45, 51
bruising 49
buttocks 17

C
calcium 21
cervical curve 14, 31
cervical placement 22, 34–35
chest complaints 18
chi 6–8, 42, 44
Chi Pilates
  anatomical terminology 10
  benefits of 9
  common questions 8–9
  definition 6
  equipment for 56
  exercises 58–93
  osteoporosis 21
  principles 22–35, 56

Chi Qong 6
childhood 21
Chinese medicine 9, 13, 41–42, 44, 48
circulation 9, 23, 51
cold feet 18
cold limbs 55
cold sores 49
colds 18, 51
communication 53
complexion 9
concentration 9, 18, 49
constipation 51
cooking 16
coughs 18, 51

D
D.I.Y. 16
death 52
diaphragm 24
diet 7, 21, 23, 47
digestion 9, 15, 48–49
disease 50
dizziness 45
double-leg stretch 47, 49, 51, 55, 78
dreaming 45
driving 16

E
earth 42, 48–49, 52
East, the 6, 7, 23, 41–58
emotional outbursts 54
energy 6–7, 13, 41–42, 45, 46, 49, 50–51, 52–53, 54
evening 50, 52
exercises
  aerobic 11, 53
  ankle circles 45, 47, 51, 55, 64
  arm circles 45, 47, 51, 93
  balance 45, 47, 49, 51, 55, 58–93
  breast stroke 47, 49, 51, 55
  double-leg stretch 47, 49, 51, 55, 78
  forward roll 47, 55, 59
  hamstring stretch 55, 81
  hip roll 45, 83
  inner thighs 47, 55, 73
  knee lifts 47, 55, 66

leg circles 51, 55, 73
leg exercises 80
leg lifts 74
lizard 45, 85
oblique 45, 49, 55, 76
press-ups 45, 47, 51, 87–88
quality of 7
regular 21
rocking 47
roll-down 49, 55, 82
roll-up 49, 51, 55, 71–72
seated twist and tilt 45, 60
shoulder bridge 45, 47, 55, 69–70
side-lying hip extension 45, 49, 79
single-leg stretch 47, 49, 55, 75
spinal flexion 55, 65
star 86
supine 10, 38, 61
swan dive 49, 51, 55, 90–91
table balance 47, 49, 92
The Hundred 47, 51, 67–68
warm-up 45, 47, 49, 51, 55, 62–63
weight-bearing 11
extension 10, 24
eyes 44–45, 55

F
family 41
fear 52, 55
female body structure 12
fibres 16, 18, 28
fire 42, 46–47, 48, 52
fitness industry 6
flexibility 9, 14, 18, 35
flexion 10, 24
flu 51
focus 42
food 7, 21, 23, 46, 48, 50, 53
forward roll 47, 55, 59
fours, on all 39
frustration 49

G
gallbladder 42, 44–45
gardening 16
genetics 21
Germany 7

green 44
grieving 51
growth 54

H
hamstring stretch 55, 81
head placement 17, 34–35
headaches 17–18
health 6, 16, 41
heart 15, 42, 46–47
heartburn 49
height gain 9
hip bones 14, 30
hip roll 45, 83
hormonal system 55
Hundred, The 47, 51, 67–68

I
illness 16
imbalance 9, 15, 17, 19, 30–31, 45, 47
immune system 9, 18, 50–51
indecision 45
information 53
injury 16
inner thighs 47, 55, 73
internal organs 12–13, 23
intervertebral discs 14
intestines 15
irritability 45, 54

J
joints 9, 16, 35, 44

K
kidneys 42, 52–55
kinesiology 14
knee lifts 47, 55, 66
kyphosis 11

L
large intestine 42, 50–51
late afternoon 52
late summer 48, 52
lateral movement 10
leg circles 51, 55, 73
leg exercises 80
leg lifts 74
lifestyle 9, 21
ligaments 16, 44
lips 49
liver 42, 44–45
lizard 45, 85
lordosis 11
lordotic curve 14, 31

94

INDEX

lumbar curve 14
lungs 9, 18, 24, 42, 50–51

M
male body structure 12
menstrual cramps 45
menstrual cycle 54
meridians 13, 41
metal 42, 48, 50–51, 52
mid-day 52
migraine 17–18
mobility 9, 35
moodiness 18
morning 52
mouth 49
movement patterns 12, 14
multiple sclerosis 45
muscles
    abdominal 17, 18, 24, 28
    abduction 10
    adduction 10
    back 17
    biceps 15
    calf 55
    cardiac 15
    concentric phase 15
    contraction 15, 16
    eccentric phase 15
    elasticity 16
    external oblique 28
    fibres 16, 18, 28
    gastrocnemius 55
    gluteus maximus 55
    hamstrings 15, 17
    hip flexors 17
    imbalance 15
    intercostal 24
    internal oblique 27, 28
    latissimus dorsi 55
    lengthening 15, 16, 21, 42
    multifidus 27, 28
    neck 34
    paraspinals 55
    pectoralis 18
    pelvic floor 27
    Pilates 8–9
    posture 12–15
    quadriceps 15, 17
    rectus abdominis 28
    skeletal 15
    smooth 15
    spine 18
    sports 28
    strengthening 53
    stretching 11, 16
    terminology 10
    transversus abdominis 27, 28–29
    trapezius 17, 18, 55
    triceps 15
musculoskeletal system 12–15

N
nails 45
neck 18, 34
nervousness 55
neurosis 51
night 52
nose 18, 49, 50
nutrients 46–47, 48, 50

O
obesity 49
oblique 45, 49, 55, 76
office work 17–18
oriental medicine 9, 13, 41–42, 44, 48
osteopathy 6, 11
osteoporosis 21
oxygen 23

P
pain 13
pelvis 11, 14, 17, 22, 24, 27–31
pericardium 42, 46–47
physiotherapy 6, 11
picking things up 16
Pilates, Joseph 7
pituitary gland 55
pollutants 50
posterior movement 10
postural positions 36–39
posture 7, 8–9, 10–11, 12–15, 16, 17–18, 19–20, 23, 35, 61
pre-menstrual tension – PMT 54
press-ups 45, 47, 51, 87–88
prolapse 49
prone, lying 10, 38
pubic bone 14

R
re-birth 52
recovery 52
red 46
relaxation 23, 42, 53
rest 52
rib cage 18, 22, 23–24, 32, 33
rocking 47
roll-down 49, 55, 82
roll-up 49, 51, 55, 71–72
rotation 10

S
sacral curve 14
sacroiliac joint 17
scapulae 17, 22, 32
scoliosis 11
seated twist and tilt 45, 60
sedentary lifestyle 21
self-destructiveness 51
self-respect 18
selfishness 18, 49
sewing 16
shiatsu 41
shoulder blades 17, 22, 32
shoulder bridge 45, 47, 55, 69–70
shoulders 18, 34
side-lying 37
side-lying hip extension 45, 49, 79
single-leg stretch 47, 49, 55, 75
sitting 37
skeleton 9, 12–15, 16, 17, 31, 35
skin complaints 47, 51
sleep 52–53
small intestine 42, 46–47
spinal flexion 55, 65
spinal pain 49
spine 10–11, 12–15, 18, 24, 27, 28, 30–31, 34–35
spirituality 41
spleen 42, 46–47, 48–49
spring 44, 48, 52
stability 22, 27, 42
standing 36
star 86
sternum 17
stomach 15, 42, 48–49
stress 9, 14, 23, 53
summer 46, 48, 52, 53
supine, lying 10, 38, 61
swan dive 49, 51, 55, 90–91
sweats 55

T
table balance 47, 49, 92
taste, sense of 47
temperature 47
tendons 16, 44
tension 18, 35
thoracic breathing 23–26
thoracic curve 14
throat 49
tongue 47, 49, 55
torso position 17, 30
toxins 47
training 16
triple heater 42, 46–47
typing 16
T'ai Chi Chuan 6, 45

U
urine 55
uterus 27

V
vertebrae 13–14
visual weakness 44–45
visualisation 29, 30

W
warm-up 45, 47, 49, 51, 55, 62–63
washing up 16
waste 46–47, 48, 55
water 42, 44, 48, 52–55
West, the 6–7, 41–58
winter 48, 52, 53
wood 42, 44–45, 48, 52
worry 49

Y
yoga 6, 53